SNOWMOBILING

THE SLEDDERS
COMPLETE HANDBOOK

DAVID HALLAM
JAMES HALLAM

Fun on Snow Publications

ISBN 0-9684018-0-5

Library of Congress Catalogue Card Number: 99-94052

Canadian Cataloging in Publication Data
Hallam Dave 1947
Snowmobiling
Hallam James 1973

GV856.5   H34   1998
796.94   C98-910827-9

Published by: Fun on Snow Publications
                        2807 Townline Road
                        Abbotsford, British Columbia,
                        Canada V2T 5E1
                        1-604-850-7381

Illustrations: Bonnie L. Ayotte
                        Vancouver, British Columbia, Canada
                        Front Cover Photo — Polaris
                        Snowmobile, Polaris Industries
                        SnowGoer USA
                        Snow Sports Canada
                        Back Cover — Polaris Snowmobile
                        Courtesy of Polaris

First Aid: St. John's Ambulance

Printed in Canada ColorCentrix Printco Ltd.

Safe Rider Logo: I.S.M.A.
International Snowmobiling Manufacturers Association

SNOWMOBILING TIPS

FOR TRAIL RIDERS &
MOUNTAIN RIDERS

- Beginners
- Intermediate
- Experienced

A Compact handbook
Fits in the trunk of your snowmobile.

- Easy Steering Setup —page 37
- Stuck Situations Page—page 42

TAKE IT WITH YOU

ABOUT THE AUTHORS

Dave and James Hallam of British Columbia Canada are the authors of this book. Dave has twenty years of trail riding and ten years mountain riding. His son James has four years trail riding and ten years mountain riding. Both, addicted to the sport, try to ride every weekend from December to May.

The locations are endless, the people are great and as Dave puts it at age fifty-one "you get younger when you are snowmobiling". James claims that he loves the sport so much he will be sledding for the rest of his life. We wonder what new sleds will look like in the future.

INTRODUCTION

This handbook is a reference tool for all sledders. It gives tips on acquiring the right machine, operation, trail and mountain riding, maintenance, troubleshooting, service techniques, survival, safety and manners on the trail.

Being the fastest growing outdoor winter sport in North America it is catching on with both old and young. Old Timers will tell you their experience with uncomfortable, noisy, unreliable and cold machines. How this has changed to the exciting machines of today that are smooth, quiet, comfortable and very reliable. Increased power, built-in warmers, and easier modes of transport have added to the ease and enjoyment of a day on the trails.

There is much to enjoy, including the social get togethers. Snowmobile clubs offer opportunities to contribute to the development of the sport. The material has been organized in quick reference format so that it can be taken along on the ride to help in a practical way.

Wherever there is snow, snowmobiling is a great way to enjoy winter. Unlimited according to age and gender, reasonable in cost, and with up to seven months of snow season in many areas, snowmobiling can take you to the inaccessible places of magnificent scenery and unspoiled nature. The back country beckons and this little book has been compiled to help open up these great possibilities for you.

DISCLAIMER

The author and FUN ON SNOW PUBLICATIONS shall have neither liability nor responsibility to any person or entity with respect to any loss or damage caused, directly or indirectly by the information contained in this book.

This book should be used only as a general guide and not as the ultimate source of Snowmobiling.

If you do not wish to be bound by the above, you may return this book to the publisher for a full refund.

TABLE OF CONTENTS

Chapter 1
YOUR FIRST SLED

Getting your first sled is when the excitement begins. When fresh powder snow stirs you, the excitement really takes off. It is time to have fun in a great sport. You will see why snowmobiling is the fastest growing outdoor sport in North America. Here are a few tips to get you started.

Choosing your sled

We suggest a 121" low profile short track, a fan cooled engine with 35 - 55 horsepower A 136" long track machine is more suited for mountain riding and not recommended for starting out on the trail.

Checking it out (Used Snowmobile)

Checklist the following, preferrably with an experienced snowmobiler:

- brakes (are pads thin?)
- compression (10% difference is allowed)
- idler wheels (loose?) or flat spots
- track lugs (damaged?)
- a bent tunnel?
- hand warmers (working?)
- carbides under skis?
- does engine start easily?
- condition of drive belt?

Where to Ride

The dealership is usually the first place to ask about safe locations. Ask about accessible, comfortable trail areas, avoiding steep slopes and isolated locations. Check with your local Snowmobile Club.

Starting to Ride (Beginners)

When you start out, keep the speed very low. Accidents often happen on the first trip out. Take it easy for two or three rides. With your left hand on the brake lever and your right hand on the throttle lever apply the throttle very gently. Be ready to squeeze the brake lever if needed. Find an area clear of fences, wires, bumps and holes (not a frozen lake) and ride around in a circle for a minimum of 2 hrs. Remember to keep the speed very low.

Tether Cord

Always attach tether cord from sled to your body. If you fall off, the engine will stop.

Registration, Licence and Insurance

Register your sled in state or province you live in. Snowmobile insurance is available for collision, theft and liability. Display licence number and decals as required. Carry registration with you.
Insurance is mandatory in most jurisdictions and is included in the registration or permit price in some provinces. Riders are usually required to carry proof of insurance on them at all times. Failure to produce evidence of insurance is regarded as not having any, and riders are fined in most places.

Getting out there

Plan your rides, be prepared, and never ride alone. Always let others know where you will be riding. Be specific about location and route.

First Sled Cost

Anywhere from $1,500.00 to $3,500.00 should get you started, for a used machine.

Riders must have zero tolerance level for drinking and snowmobiling

---

Sled Renting

If you pick up the sled it is approximately $125.00 to $200.00 per day. If you are staying at a lodge, the cost can drop to about $75.00 to $100.00 per day. A damage deposit is usually required.

Courses (New Snowmobiler)

For the new snowmobiler, some Snowmobiling Associations offer safe riding courses to get you started. We recommend you take a safe riding course, if you have never ridden a snowmobile or are a beginner. Remember safety always comes first.

Spare Drive Belt

Always carry a spare drive belt.

Chapter 2

CLOTHING

Clothing that keeps you safe and comfortable ranks as a top priority for having fun in the outdoors. If you are not dressed warmly, a whole day of the sport can be spoiled. The weather can change, emergencies can happen.

Helmet, Sun Glasses, Shield

Definitely use government approved helmets, preferrably one with a face shield, a tinted shield or sunglasses in daylight riding. In extremely cold, below -20C shields ice up. Electric plug-in heaters actually do work, keeping shield ice free. Always wear your helmet. Do not wear a tinted helmet shield at dusk or dark.

Gloves

All-leather box finger gloves, preformed sewn fingers, are warm, but in extreme cold, all-leather mitts are best. For agile riders thin gloves give better control.

The Neck

Use a neckie, it goes on and off easily. The neckie protects the front and back of your neck from cold air. If you don't have it on, the cold air travels the shape of the helmet and you can soon get a cold neck.

Bib Pants and Jacket

Use windproof material for sure, and waterproof, if you can. Layer your clothing so that trapped air between garments can act as insulation. Try in this order:

- underwear next to skin
- a shirt over underwear
- a polar fleece jacket over the shirt
- bib pants over the fleece
- a windproof jacket over bib pants
- don't wear cotton
- try polyester blend

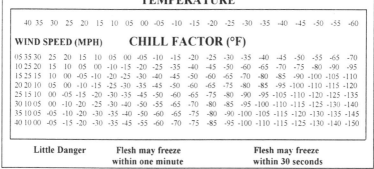

WIND CHILL: HOW COLD IS IT?

To determine the wind chill factor on your next ski trip,
find the box where the current wind speed and temperature intersect.

TEMPERATURE

40	35	30	25	20	15	10	05	00	-05	-10	-15	-20	-25	-30	-35	-40	-45	-50	-55	-60

WIND SPEED (MPH)   **CHILL FACTOR (°F)**

WIND SPEED																				
05	35	30	25	20	15	10	05	00	-05	-10	-15	-20	-25	-30	-35	-40	-45	-50	-55	-65	-70
10	25	20	15	10	05	00	-10	-15	-20	-25	-35	-40	-45	-50	-60	-65	-70	-75	-80	-90	-95
15	25	15	10	00	-05	-10	-20	-25	-30	-40	-45	-50	-60	-65	-70	-80	-85	-90	-100	-105	-110
20	20	10	05	00	-10	-15	-25	-30	-35	-45	-50	-60	-65	-75	-80	-85	-95	-100	-110	-115	-120
25	15	10	00	-05	-15	-20	-30	-35	-45	-50	-60	-65	-75	-80	-90	-95	-105	-110	-120	-125	-135
30	10	05	00	-10	-20	-25	-30	-40	-50	-55	-65	-70	-80	-85	-95	-100	-110	-115	-125	-130	-140
35	10	05	-05	-10	-20	-30	-35	-40	-50	-60	-65	-75	-80	-90	-100	-105	-115	-120	-130	-135	-145
40	10	00	-05	-15	-20	-30	-35	-45	-55	-60	-70	-75	-85	-95	-100	-110	-115	-125	-130	-140	-150

Little Danger	**Flesh may freeze within one minute**	**Flesh may freeze within 30 seconds**

Footwear

You will find that tight fitting boots with thick socks are colder than loose fitting boots with thinner socks. Use waterproof boots with double wool liners, or polypropylene sock liners and wool socks or solar fleece socks with aluminum reflector liners.

Chemical Warmers

Shake these until they get warm and then drop them into gloves, boots, etc.

7.2 nights per snowmobile season that snowmobilers spend in a motel/resort room while sledding.

Chapter 3

TRANSPORTING YOUR SLED

Transporting sleds is part of the effort that has to be put out for the joy of the sport. So here are a few tips to get you out and back safely without damage to the equipment.

Using a Pickup Truck

This is the simplest method. A plywood ramp with rungs enables one person to get the sled on and off but it is expected that you are meeting friends at the riding area.

Sled-Deck

This fits on a regular pickup box and carries two sleds. It is compact and includes a pull out ramp.

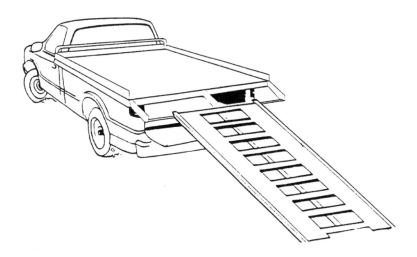

Sled Trailer

An 8' wide by 10' long is designed to carry two sleds. Get a tilt deck, 13" wheels spin a little slower than 10", so bearings may last longer.

Drive On -Drive Off

These trailers save your back. They are quite effective in that they are drive on - drive off with the front ramps acting as a slush guard when trailering. Available in 2, 4 and 6 sled models.

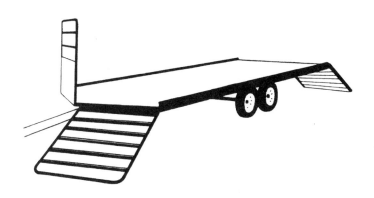

Sled Placement

Position the sled's weight in front of the axle to get the weight on the tongue, otherwise the wrongly placed weight will yank on the hitch. Trailer will sway if weight is at back.

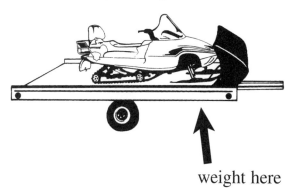

weight here

The Cube Van

You will need a ramp, but a 16' will carry two large sleds and one small sled put in backwards. No need to tie down, cinch, or cover your machines. A 220 mile round trip in a rental, can cost as low as $200.00 including fuel, mileage and rent fee. Split three ways it may be worth saving all the hassle of trailering and cleanup.

Safety Chains & Lights (Trailer)

Attach safety chains tight allowing only enough play to turn. Cross the chains underneath the hitch. Double check chains and lights.

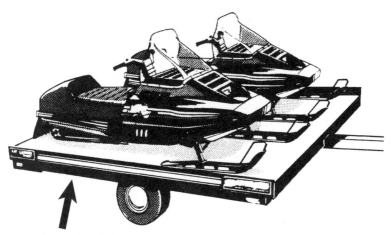

Put cinch here

Cinches

Recommended are heavy duty cinches, 8,000 lbs capacity put through the skid frame of both sleds on the trailer. The cinch ends clip nicely under the trailer edge lip. This holds the rear end of the sleds down tight. But be sure you secure the skis as well.

Wheels (Tires)

Using a bearing packer, repack the bearings every season. Less than 2 mm of tread means new tires are needed.

Trailer Maintenance

Put a lubricant up under the coupler, attach to ball and tighten adjustment nut enough to reduce play. Do not over tighten. In checking wheel nuts, loosen first and then tighten.

Sled Covers (Nylon Canvas)

Using sled covers keeps machines clean and dry and also stops a possible broken hood if wind catches it.

Broken Hoods

Don't transport your snowmobiles in a pickup or trailer backwards. The hood can fly open resulting in approximately $800.00 bill.

Fuel Off (Sled)

Shut the fuel off while trailering and when the sled is parked on an incline. Gas can leak into the intake of the sled causing a possible flooded engine.

Trailer Covers (Fibreglass)

These covers usually made of aluminum or fiberglass are a good idea. They protect your sled from rain, salt, sand and wind on the highway.

False Bottom

You can make a false bottom in your pickup truck box to store your pullout ramp. This way you will not have to stand it up beside your sled. Tie your sled down tight.

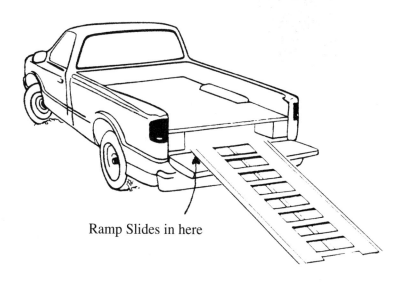

Ramp Slides in here

41 is the median age of snowmobile owners.

Quick, Light and Easy (Ramps)

These are usually designed for a pickup truck and made of aluminum. Cost is approximately $200.00 to $250.00.

Chapter 4

TRAIL RIDING

Handling, and Suspension Adjustments

These topics go hand in hand and as you tinker with your suspension adjustments you quickly learn it affects the way your sled handles.

Trail Sled

A good trail sled is equipped with approximately 500 to 600cc liquid cooled engine, a 40" ski stance low centre of gravity, 15" x 121" track .75 to 1" lugs and decent biting carbides, 4" to 6" in length.

Touring Sleds

Generally used for smooth trails. They have all the bells and whistles. Track is 136" long. The seat accommodates two people. Passenger hand warmers and holders, along with a passenger back rest is usually standard.

Fluid Check

Top up gas, antifreeze and injection oil before riding. Always use a good, clean container for fueling. When pouring fuel into sled gas tank, use a clean funnel equipped with a fine screen. Make sure snowmobile is turned off before fuelling. Check chain case oil level.

Centre of Gravity (CG)

Keep your body low going in and out of corners. Back off on the throttle a little, when going into the curve and throttle up coming out. Always lean into the corner.

Parking

When stopping on the trail, pull over to let the other sledders by. Remember, on snow the edge of the bank looks farther away than it is. Always ride on the right hand side of the trail.

Pivoting

Pivoting is caused when the front skid spring and shock are too tight, pressing down on the front of track and skid. Loosen front shock and spring of rear suspension and shorten limiter strap, to get the front of the track off the ground just a little.

Fishtailing

This condition means more traction is needed on the track. A few studs can help. Get the track up a bit at track front by shortening limiter strap.

Numbness in the Hands

Caused by vibration or bouncing front suspension or a vibrating engine. Tighten front springs and check for worn shocks. Also, you can try stronger rated springs in front suspension.Worn jackshaft bearings will cause vibration.

Ski Push (Understeer)

This describes skis that drift or push snow in corners. Try more ski pressure or more aggressive skis.

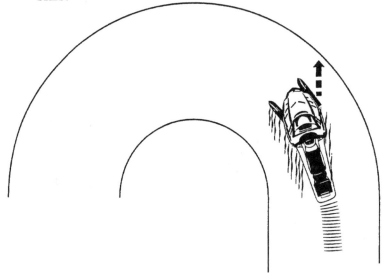

Too much rear traction or not enough carbide up front. Too many studs or too agressive studs will cause understeer.

Loose Condition (Oversteer)

This happens with non-aggressive track when the rear of sled comes around to overtake the skis. Try matching aggressive skis with aggressive track.

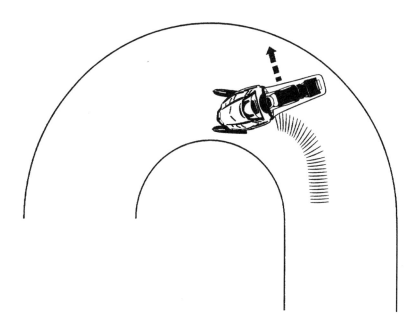

Too much carbide up front or not enough rear end traction. Increase studs.

Set up

It takes trial and error to get it right for your riding style. But the right set up matched to a good sled is what you are striving for.

Fuel Gauge

Keep your eye on the fuel gauge and remember to turn around when it reads just over half full, unless you are carrying an extra supply.

Steering Effort

Get the steering feeling as light as possible without affecting sled turning and handling. Wrestling hard steering will leave you with aching shoulders and sore muscles for a few days. (see page 37)

Following

Following the rider ahead too closely can cause a damaging accident. Without braking, all he has to do is let off the throttle, and his sudden halt can lead to a hit.

Free Horsepower

The aim is to reduce rolling resistance by removing as much friction as possible. The key causes include, too much tension on the drive chain, tracks that are too tight, or metal skis that are sticking. Manufacturers continue to work out these areas of friction.

Sustaining your Energy

Take along a good supply of water. Perhaps included a sport drink for mineral and salt replacement. Avoid starchy, sugary treats because more solid foods will keep your energy up for full enjoyment of the day.

Fuel

Get good clean gas. Choose a high traffic station to insure fresh, moisture free fuel. Owners manual will recommend the correct octane and/or regular or premium fuel. Use a funnel with a fine screen.

Food

For hot snacks strap a hot dogger cooker on the exhaust pipe, throw in sausages or pre-made dinners wrapped in foil. A supply of granola bars, beef or chicken sandwiches is always good to have. Remember, caffein drinks and chocolate are diuretics and not good for strenuous riding.

There are 220,000 miles of groomed and marked trails in NorthAmerica

Ski-Alignment

Get the inside of the skis parallel with the out-side edge of the track. Use a straight edge along the outside track edge up past the inside ski. With bars straight, measure between the front part of the ski to straight edge and rear part of the ski to straight edge. Use a bungie cord to keep front skis taut. With the skis now parallel to the track, toe each ski tip out (away from the centerline of the machine). Distance "A" should be 3mm (1/8") to 6mm (1/4") greater than the "B" when you're done.

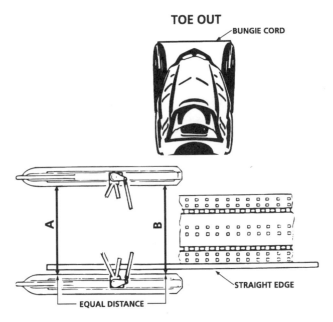

Adjust ski alignment by rotating the tie rod.

Darting

Make sure ski alignment is correct. Have track flat on the ground, carbides and wear bar in really good shape. If front of skis are toed in, front of sled will dart. Less ski pressure can decrease darting combined with less aggressive keel skis. When riding on hard packed snow, the ski wear bars may want to follow existing runner tracks in the snow. The more weight on the skis and the more aggressive the wear bar on the ski, the more the skis will want to steer themselves or "dart". Reducing weight on the skis by increasing spring preload on the front arm of the track suspension and lengthening the limiter strap will reduce darting. Removing one carbide runner and replacing it with a standard runner can help reduce darting as well.

Hooker Handles

These are usually for the more aggressive rider. They aid in turning and add good control. Installed in handle bar end, they are great for trails.

Handle Balls

These fit nicely into the end of sled's handle bars. You can really get a grip with these trick add-ons. Aids in stopping your hands from slipping off the end of handle bar while trail riding.

Track Winch (Tight Spots)

You can pull your sled out with a rope tied to the front windows of the track. Carry 50' -75' of 3/8" rope. Once tied to the holes in your track and then secured to a tree, other sled, rock or several people, start your motor and throttle it out very gently.

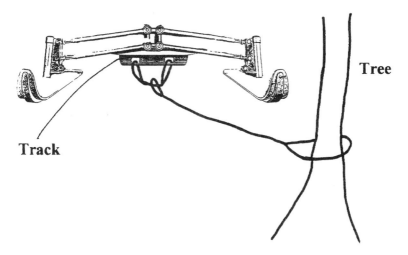

Tree

Track

Injection Oil Timing (it can fool you)

If your throttle cable has been stretched, the injection oil timing that matches fuel flow will produce symptoms that you can miss. The engine has lower power, wet plugs, runs rich, and is extremely hard to start. It is a problem easily overlooked when out on the trail. Check your pump timing yearly.

Group Riding (Safari Riding)

- Always abide by Snomobiler's code of ethics. Courtesy. *(See Page 116)*
- Don't let yourself be pressured to drive beyond your ability.
- Never pass the leader
- Stay in line
- Maintain 100 feet minimum between sleds while moving.
- Extreme caution at intersections.
- Always watch the sled in front of you.
- Each rider repeat hand signals given by the leader or the rider ahead of him. *(See Page 113)*

Adjusting Rear Suspension

There are usually 3 to 4 settings for ride comfort on rear of suspension. The settings also affect ski pressure. The front and rear arms of the track suspension system generally have preload adjusters for the springs on them. Adding more preload on the front arm will take pressure off the skis softening the preload on the front arm and adding preload to the springs on the rear arm will increase ski pressure. Be careful not to get the ride too soft since it will bottom out the sled on moguls or jumps. You could bend something like tunnel or blow shocks.

Adjusting Front Suspension

Most modern sleds have coil springs over shocks. Tighten by shortening the spring. This adds ski pressure and more responsive steering. Softening or lengthening the spring reduces ski pressure and makes it easier to turn the sled. Be careful not to set too soft since the front may bounce and this takes more rider input to control.

Easy Steering Set-up

You can have easy steering. Adjust front suspension springs as soft as possible. Set rear of rear suspension on the softest setting. Rocker keel skis can help. Lengthen limiter strap accordingly and be careful not to lengthen too much as sled can pivot. Easy turn steering pivot also reduces effort by as much as 20%.

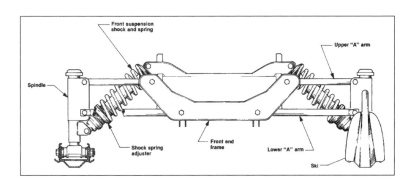

Arctic Cat front suspension

Polaris Front suspension.
Typical trailing arm type.

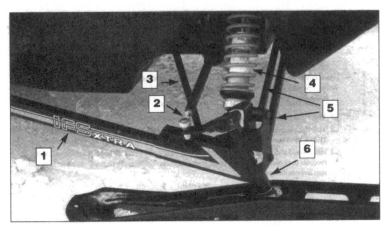

1. Trailing arm; 2. Tie-rod or steering rod; 3. Anti-sway or torsion bar; 4. Shock and spring; 5. Radius rods; 6. Ski spindle.

Anti-Sway Bar

Don't adjust this too tight, or the sled can dart and be difficult to drive.

Shocks

After first shock rebuild, a general rule of thumb for service intervals is every 2000 to 2500 miles or every year, depending on how much you ride. This may sound too often to some, but is necessary. Some key signs that may tip you off to a shock that needs to be serviced include:

- a very soft or flat feel in ride quality
- on take off from a jump, the snowmobile consistently rotates to the same side.
- after riding, the snowmobile appears lower in ride height. Also, one side may appear higher than the other.
- on visual inspection, you notice oil around the shock and or a rust appearance on the shock shaft.
- a very springy feeling over hills and jumps.
- the snowmobile has suddenly picked up a severe understeer or oversteer condition.

These are just some signs to help you pick out a possible shock problem that may be hampering ride quality.

It is important not to overlook servicing your shocks because they are an integral part of how your snowmobile rides.

Parts and Add-Ons

Consult the local Snowmobile dealer or Snowmobile magazines for items described in this book.

Chapter 5
MOUNTAIN RIDING

The lure of the mountains is to ride over fresh untracked mountain powder on a beautiful day.

Mountain Sled

A good mountain sled is equipped with a 500 to 600cc liquid cooled engine 15" x 136" track with 1.5 - 2" deep lug track, altitude compensators, mountain bar, gas rack, and 37 - 38" ski stance.

Stuck Sled

Have one or two people tug on the ski loops, walk beside the sled while you gently apply the throttle. This should succeed nine out of ten times.

Badly stuck Sled

Keep cool. Get all the snow out of your suspension and point sled down hill. Try turning sled around -180° Pack down a twenty foot strip, sled width. Don't pin the throttle, it could dig you in deeper. Once it lifts out, use all of your riding skills to keep it moving. Remember, hot clutches will cause belt slippage. Let these parts cool down before riding out. If stuck in deep snow try this: just roll the sled completely over

Author's Log Cabin in Snow Country

Side Hilling

Practice makes perfect and this technique takes a few tries before you get it right. Always lean to the upside of the hill. Give a generous tug on the grab bar and a handful of the throttle.

Towing in Deep Snow

Get the towed sled as close as possible to the bumper of the towing sled. Use two to three sleds to help tow one sled. Carry 50 - 100 ft. of nylon rope.

Cooler Temperatures

If you are stuck in the bottom of a bowl consider waiting till the snow firms up and the sun goes down. The temperature drop provides better traction for climbing out. (own risk only). Don't go down where you can't get out.

High Marking

Get ready to turn around if needed. Calculate your return before you go up. This takes practice, and applies only to riders with lots of experience.

Spring Riding

This is the time of year there may be a good base and maybe 6" of powder. You can go so many places. Riding becomes a "point and shoot" sled day.

Track-Footprint

Drop the suspension out of the tunnel as far as possible to get as much track on the ground as possible.

Climbing

Stand on the back of the running boards to increase traction. Get your body weight slightly forward to stop sled from flipping over backwards.

Stop Switch

An engine switch that accidentally shuts off by bumping it with your hand gets you into real trouble. Keep hands and knees away from stop switch while climbing.

Power Band

The wider the power band, the more forgiving it is for mountains. Peaky engine power is more difficult to clutch.

Limiter Strap (Mountains)

Lengthen the limiter strap and increase the tension of the front skid spring. Quick adjusting straps are great. The longer the strap the more ski lift, the shorter the strap the less ski lift.

Revving RPM (Drive Clutch)

In the drive clutch, if the engine is over-revving install heavier weights. If it is under-revving use lighter weights. If you are into fine tuning on the mountain look to adjustable weights. Keep an eye on the tachometer. To bring top RPM's down a higher angle helix can be used in back clutch.

Ski-Doo's TRA clutch design incorporates three external adjusters that allow fine tuning of the shift speed of the pulley. There are six adjustment positions, each allowing a change of 150 to 200 RPM (see pages 72, 78)

Low End Bogging

Drop carb pilot jets a couple of sizes. Install weights in drive clutch with an <u>engagement notch</u>. Try higher pretension spring in the drive clutch. Raise idle RPM to approximately 2,800 RPMS.

Handlebars

Install handlebar riser approximately 2" and a mountain grab bar. Having a mountain bar to aid side-hilling is a must.

Mountain Bars

There are a few types of mountain bars. Basically the metal type and the softer bolt-on type. The soft add-on's are easier on your ribs in case you come down too hard after a jump.

Metal replaces stock bars.

Softer add-on type no need to change bars.

Grippers

There is a lot of stand up riding in the mountains. Install some type of running board grippers such as sandpaper peel and stick or metal screws 4" apart, or grip plates.

Backshift (Downshift)

Try a smaller degree angle helix in back clutch. This can improve downshift. A straight angle helix is preferrable.

When the rider sees a challenging hill ahead, he expects a lightning quick downshift.

Compass

Carry a map of the area and a compass and know how to use the compass.

Altitude Headaches

Use an altimeter and stop climbing at about 5000 to 6000 feet to climatize your heart, lungs and head, or when you start feeling light headed.

Rear Suspension (Climbing)

Set rear of rear suspension to stiffest position. This can help you climb better and maintain control.

Fuel Anti-Freeze

Freezing anywhere in the fuel system can cause major problems and de-icers should always be used. Many states in the US have mandated the use of "oxygenated" gasoline, however. If the fuel you're using is already oxygenated, you don't need to add any additional de-icers. If your fuel is not oxygenated, add 4 ounces of isopropyl alcohol per tank for insurance.

80% of snowmobile accidents in North America are alchohol related.

Getting down

Use two spare belts by dropping them over the ski tips and up against the spindles with belt ends under the skis. These act as extra brakes. Also plastic chains from hardware store.

High Mark Advantage

When wanting to do the high mark take the hill on an angle instead of straight up. This cuts the angle steepness down for your sled.

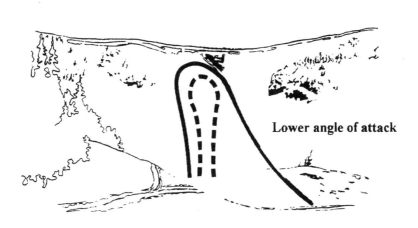

Lower angle of attack

CAUTION! May Trigger Avalanche!

High Engagement (Causing Stuck Situations)

If you are engaging the sled to high RPM, eg. 5000 to 5400 RPM and are getting stuck, most likely you are getting a too quick track spin, and breaking the track loose. We tested this with two identical sleds, identical tracks. One engaged at 3,200 RPM, the other at 5,200 RPM. Time after time we dug out the 5,200 RPM sled.

Altitude Compensators

Some mountain sleds come stock with altitude compensators. They work well and can reduce the need for jet changes.

Getting at the Jet (Bottom of carb)

Main jet will be revealed when the nut cap is removed. Use a 6mm socket on main jet for most Mikuni carbs.

Hooker Handles

These are usually for a little more aggressive rider to aid in turning and add better control. Install in handle bar ends. The smaller type can aid in side hilling.

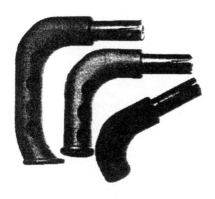

Stabilizer Bar

Stablilizer bar or anti-roll bar works to keep the sled flatter. Too much tension on this bar can cause darting and driving difficulties. Removing the stabilizer bar gets the front suspension to work independently and a lot of mountain riders take them out to aid in side hilling

Lower Gearing

For those who want to climb a little higher on the mountain. Drop 1-2 gears in the chaincase (a great help). Lower gearing also helps clutch heating problems as well as throttle response. This gives sled a quick light feel. Chain case is on throttle side. Top gear fits on Jack Shaft.

Top gear fits on jack shaft.

Lower gear fits on drive axle.

Hill climb.

Chapter 6

JETTING & ALTITUDE

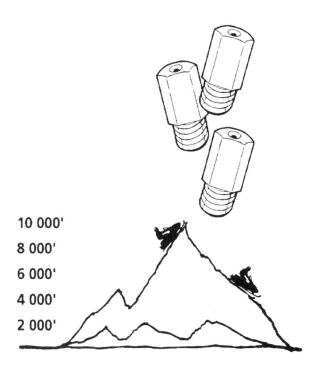

Altitude greatly affects snowmobile engines. As a carbureted sled climbs in elevation it looses 3% of HP for every 1000 feet it climbs. Re-calibration can be done to help counter this loss of power. High altitude kits include changes to carb, clutch and gearing. When going up in elevation, the carb gets less air causing the engine to run a richer mixture, getting too much gas for the air it is receiving. This calls for a carb re-jet. Over 4000 feet elevation a high altitude kit is recommended.

Jetting (Definition)

The term used to describe the calibration of fuel and air mixture supplied by carburetor. By use of a carburetor, main jet, pilot jet, needle jet, jet needle, slide cutaway and air screw adjustments.

Jetting simplified (Ascending)

Start with a sea level main jet installation. This should work fine riding around less than 4000 feet elevation. Above that level re-jetting may become necessary, depending on how high you ride as well as the sled you ride. If your engine starts to sputter and stops as you climb then drop one size main jet for every 2000 feet altitude. For example; if the jet you remove reads 280, try a 270 jet. If the engine is still not crisp drop to 260. These numbers would be different for different model sleds. If altitude compensators are being used rejetting can be reduced. These are therefore recommended, provided that the compensator has the correct main jet installed for sea level.

Descending Elevation

As you come down in altitude go up one jet size for every 2000 feet descended. Remember, where you changed your last jet going up, and change back at this point, or burn down can occur.

Sea Level

Most sleds come out of the box with a sea level set up. Ascending more than 4000 feet does require a high altitude kit, which can be obtained at most dealers.

Altitude Compensators

Some mountain sleds come stock with altitude compensators. They work well and can reduce the need for jet changes.

Getting at the Jet

Main jet will be revealed when the nut cap is removed. Use a 6mm socket on main jet.

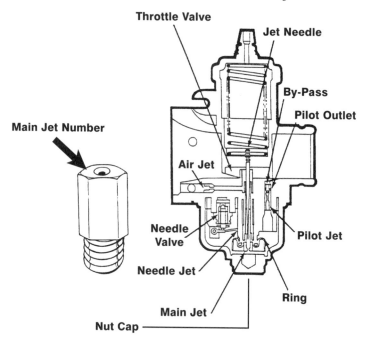

Throttle Valve

Jet Needle

By-Pass

Pilot Outlet

Main Jet Number

Air Jet

Needle Valve

Pilot Jet

Needle Jet

Main Jet

Ring

Nut Cap

Main Jet

This jet regulates the fuel supplied at 3/4 to wide open throttle, maximum RPM and horsepower. The larger the main jet, the more fuel is supplied. Rule of thumb as you go up in altitude go down in the jet size. As you go down in altitude go up in jet size.

Jet Number

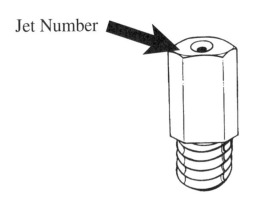

Pocket Tuner

If you are quite interested in carb jetting, pick up the inexpensive pocket tuner from Mikuni. Dealer should have them

SLIDE RULE DESIGN - Mikuni Pocket Tuner

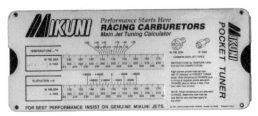

The pocket tuner has been developed to answer common questions and assist in proper jet selection. The pocket tuner will determine the main jet necessary for changes in temperature or elevation. For carbs with up to 540 main jets in use.

Chapter 7

ENGINE CARBS & PLUG CHECK

Keeping these components well maintained can make your day. Kicking snow at your sled in frustration can be avoided by tuning them in your shop.

Engine

Always warm up liquid cooled engine 2 - 3 minutes and 1 - 2 minutes for fan cooled engines before riding.

Engine Timing

Although snowmobile engines do not go out of time often, a good idea is to have the dealer check it when your sled is in for another repair.

Sparkplugs

Start the season with a new set of plugs. Check these new plugs for spark. Gap plugs to snowmobile manufacturer's specs.

Two-Stroke Oil

Run high quality injection oil, the oil prefereably from the dealer.

Compression

Compression tells the story of the basic condition of your engine. Using a compression tester, note the readings for each cylinder and compare them with shop manual specification, 110-150 is good. If one cylinder is 110 and another 140 there is a problem. A 10% window is allowed. Be sure to hold the throttle wide open when cranking to test pressure. Consult dealer for correct compression for the engine you are testing.

500cc. The most popular engine size of recently acquired snowmobiles is in this range.

Motor Mounts

These do loosen up. Check and tighten when this happens.

Air Cooled Engine Fan Belt.

Be sure this belt is in top condition. A junk belt can break and leave you stranded. Best to carry a spare new belt.

Antifreeze (Engines) Batteries (Water)

The minerals and impurities contained in some tap water are harmful to batteries and will reduce the service life of a battery. Tap water may react with cooling system metals and cause corrosion or build up of deposits that reduce cooling system efficiency and flow. Don't use straight anti-freeze in engine. Rather, use either a 50/50 or 60/40 mix of anti-freeze (or coolant) and distilled water, depending on the freeze protection for your area.

Bunged Main Jet

It is difficult to get a bunged main jet in the carb. Use Mikuni Jets only in Mikuni Carbs. Carry new main jets as spares.

Air Box and Foam Air Filter

When filter gets dirty it restricts air to the engine reducing performance. Wash with soap and water, and dry out at home. If icing up occurs in foam filter, shake out.

Air Screw

This meters airflow into carb. In is less air and out is more air on Mikunis.

In Line Filter (Fuel)

Put a new one of these on your gas line every year.

Servicing Carburetors

Before the season starts, remove the carbs, dismantle, and clean parts thoroughly with carb cleaner and forced air.

Water Traps

Shut off gas flow and remove water traps. Empty them and replace the trap under carb.

Cracked Flanges

Check carb flanges for cracks and check if carb clamps are tight. With engine running, spray carb cleaner around flanges and clamps. If you hear a marked difference in RPM, you could have an air leak. Work on it till you get it air tight.

Don't Switch Carbs

If carbs are removed, make sure they are returned to the same intake position as before.

Brittle Fuel Lines

Replace fuel lines that are getting old and brittle.

Kinked Lines

When fuel lines are too long and routed through a maze of carb bodies, etc., they can get hidden kinks and cause reduced gas feed. Try to shorten the route and therefore the line.

Carb Synchronization

To get carb slides coming up at the same time adjust the nut on top of the carbs. Look into both carb throats at same time. Depress throttle. If one carb slide comes up before the other, carbs are not synchronized. The carburetor slides should be perfectly synchronized on any multi-carb setup. Adjustment varies depending upon the design of the carbs but an adjustment is always provided. "Racked" carbs operated by a single shaft, are easily adjusted and stay in adjustment once set. Individually cable operated versions require more frequent attention. The trick is to get all slides to lift exactly together, clear the bore completely when the thumb control is wide open and to adjust the oil pump cable to its proper idle position. It is often easiest to use a mirror to watch the throttle slides when performing these adjustments. Be sure to set your idle speed before setting the oil pump idle position.

Spark Plug check

Make sure your engine is at full operating temperature. A plug check determines how well your jetting is tuned to your engine for current conditions, at a specific RPM. Find an open, unrestricted area without rocks, fences, or big bumps. On full throttle have engine pull hard for 500 feet. (Shut off engine) Keep throttle on, grab brake and come to a stop. Do not let engine run at all as this will give an incorrect plug reading. Pull spark plugs and verify color electrodes. Black and oily means too rich, light coffee brown with cream is a correct reading, white to light means the mixture is too lean.

Pipes (Be Aware)

Adding aftermarket pipes for more horsepower should be done by a competent pipe installer. There are carb jet changes, etc. involved. You can actually have less horsepower than stock if not done correctly.

Black Oily Plug

Appearance indicates jetting is too rich. Go down one jet size at a time until you get that coffee color.

Creamed Coffee Brown (Tan)

This is what you want. If you have been changing jets, pat yourself on the back for peak performance.

White

This is a problem waiting to happen and could be on the way to a burn down. Jetting too lean. Go up one jet size at a time until you get that coffee color

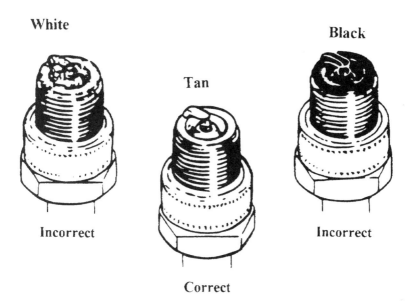

White

Black

Tan

Incorrect

Incorrect

Correct

ENGINE CONDITION TOO RICH
SYMPTOMS:

a. Performance is flat, not crisp.

b. Condition is worse when engine is hot.

c. Condition is worse when the choke/starter is used.

d. Dark, fouled spark plug.

e. Removal of air cleaner helps

f. Exhaust popping or backfire.

g. Engine sound is dull.

ENGINE CONDITION TOO LEAN
SYMPTOMS:

a. Acceleration poor, surging.

b. Performance improves slightly as engine warms.

c. Better performance when choke/starter is used.

d. No color, overheated spark plug electrode.

e. Removal of air cleaner makes condition worse.

f. Popping back through carburetor.

g. Engine pings or knocks, excessive engine heat.

Rich Jetting
Too much fuel.

Lean Jetting
Not enough fuel.

Temperature

As the temperature drops the air is more dense. This may require you to jet up. A rising temperature that reduces density can require you to jet down. Develop a feel for your carb and always do a plug check.

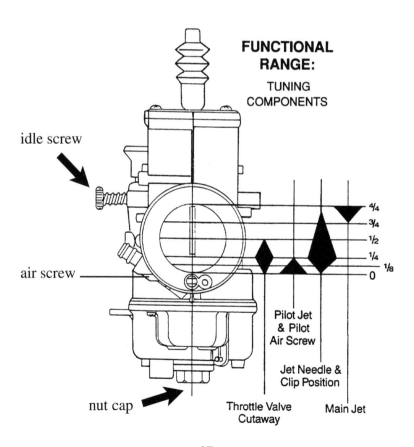

FUNCTIONAL
RANGE:

TUNING
COMPONENTS

idle screw

air screw

nut cap

Pilot Jet
& Pilot
Air Screw

Jet Needle &
Clip Position

Throttle Valve
Cutaway

Main Jet

⁴/₄
³/₄
¹/₂
¹/₄
¹/₈
0

Chapter 8
CLUTCHES & BELTS

The clutches are the heart of the snowmobile. Good clutch calibration improves efficiency and performance. There are two clutches on the snowmobile. One is drive, front or primary. The other is called the driven clutch, the secondary, or back clutch. We refer to them as clutches but technically they are pulleys.

Drive Clutch & Engagement

The drive pulley or clutch, is a centrifugally governed, variable diameter pulley. Flyweights in the pulley generate centrifugal force which is controlled by ramps and rollers. An axial component of the centrifugal force is used to push against a return spring. The ramps, rollers and spring are cali-

69

brated to provide a normal engagement speed of about 4000 RPM. This is the RPM at which the pulley will squeeze the belt and begin transferring torque from the engine to the belt.

A spring with a higher preload will force the clutch to engage at a higher RPM, a softer spring at a lower RPM. A spring with a higher rate will also cause the shift speed to increase, allowing the engine to run at a higher RPM. Stiffer springs are normally used for high elevations and are included in high altitude set up kits.

Driven Clutch

The driven pulley receives torque from the engine via the drive belt. The fixed length drive belt is drawn down into the driven pulley as the drive pulley closes. The upshift will continue until the torque load on the drive axle, which is driving the track, exceeds the torque transmitted by the driven pulley to the axle. The cam on the driven pulley will literally "screw" the driven pulley back to a lower ratio. The angle on the cam has the most effect on the shifting speed of the driven pulley but small adjustments can be made by changing the preload on the driven pulley spring. The end of the spring can be placed in one of several locations to change the prelcad. Higher preload will slow the upshift and speed the downshift, causing the RPM to increase, Dropping the preload will speed the upshift and slow the downshift, lowering the RPM and loading the engine more.

Back Shifting

Quicker back shifting can be obtained by using a lower degree helix. Example: Go down in degrees from 53 to 49. Different sleds require different angle cams (Helix). Higher spring preload will speed the back shift.

Up Shifting

Quicker up shifts can be obtained by using a steeper angle helix. An example: Go up in degrees from 49 to 53 degrees. Lower spring preload will speed the upshift.

Clutch Balance

Be sure they are balanced, since unbalanced clutches can damage their internal parts and also cause unwanted vibration.

Cooling Clutches

A vent tube can be installed in front of the sled to direct cold air onto the clutches. Make sure snow is filtered out. Lower gearing can help in chain case for clutch cooling. Windage plates added to streamline the driven pulley should be removed for mountain riding.

Clutch Rattle

A serious chatter means you should get home and have it inspected for a rebuild.

Cleaning Clutches

Before season starts completely dismantle and clean both clutches since belt dust builds up. Use compressed air to blow them out every 500 - 1000 miles.

Trail Tuning

Install a higher angle helix than stock in the driven pulley. This can smooth out the power for flat groomed trails. (personal preference).

Mountain Tuning

Install a lower angle helix than stock in the back clutch and a higher preload than stock drive clutch spring. If over rev occurs try heavier weights in drive clutch. If under rev occurs try lighter weights. (personal preference). Ski-Doos TRA clutch design incorporates three external adjusters that allow fine tuning of the shaft speed of the pulley. There are six adjustment positions, each allowing a change of 150 to 200 RPM.

Clutch Overheating (Belts)

HEAT is the worst enemy for a belt. When deep powder puts demands on clutches they get hot. so hot that they glaze the belt and it slips. When this happens, let them cool down and change the belt. The spare belt should not be a junker. Lower gearing assists in keeping clutches cooler.

Clutch Alignment

Have a competent mechanic align the clutches.

Clutch Guards

Do not run clutches with the clutch guard off. Exploding clutch can cause serious injury.

Spare Parts (these can break)

Carry an extra drive spring, driven spring, and helix (cam). Always carry a spare drive belt.

Drive Clutch Spring   Helix   Driven Clutch Spring

Take these along. They can break.
Tools needed: Clutch puller, breaker bar, torque wrench, socket set, and allen wrenches.

Black Streaks

These streaks on the drive clutch indicate your belt has been slipping. Check driven pressure preload drive pulley calibration and clutch alignment.

Soft Compound Belts

These drive belts have excellent clutch gripping characteristics.

Hard Compound Belts

These are designed for big horsepower and high altitude riding.

Ruined Belts

The causes for this are as follows: worn out belts, super hot clutches, misaligned clutches and high horsepower not matched to belt, engagement RPM too high, flat spotting due to tracks frozen to ground.

Belt Deflection

This is the amount you can push down on the middle of the belt with the motor off. The recommended deflection is 1 and 1/4 inch. If deflection is sloppy, say 2-3 inches, the clutches will not work well.

Belt Dust

Surplus dust is a sign something is out of line or the belt cannot handle the demands of the clutches. A little is common and unless there seems to be an excessive amount don't worry.

Clutch Rule

To change engine speed RPM, work with drive clutch. To improve back shift, work with driven pulley.

Cogged Belts

All belts are cogged but some belts are ribbed on the outer side. The idea behind this is to have them run cooler.

Wear Limit

As drive belts wear, they lose width. The narrower a belt becomes, the further the drive pulley must close to grip it and the larger the radius the belt will be when the pulley contacts the belt. It's like trying to start out in second gear. Some compensation is provided for belt wear with the driven pulley. Adjustment screws or shims between the halves allow the driven pulley to close further than normal. Adjustment is made while checking for

1,200. Number of miles the average snowmobiler rides per year.

proper belt deflection. When a drive belt has lost 1/8" of its original width, it must be replaced and the driven pulley opened back up for the new wider belt.

Clutch Identification

Drive Clutch	Driven Pulley
Primary Clutch	Secondary Pulley
Front Clutch	Back Pulley

Chain Tension (Chain Case)

If your chain has a manual tensioner you can check it without removal of the chain case cover. Grab the driven pulley (with belt off) and rotate from forward and back. If sloppy, say 1/2 to 1 inch it is probably too loose. Retention to approximately 1/4 inch play.

Removing Clutch Easily

It is much easier to remove a warm clutch than a cold one. Warm means clutch running time is 10 minutes or more.

Drive Clutch Weights

The majority of modern clutches have three clutch weights, and some drive clutches have four. Along with drive spring, they determine how engagement occurs and the top RPM desired. The shape or profile determines smooth roll on acceleration or hard aggressive shifting pattern. There are a multitude of curves, shapes, profiles, notches and weights. They are also called drive clutch cam arms.

T.R.A. Clutch (Ski-Doo only)

The T.R.A. total range adjustable clutch from Ski-doo is somewhat different from Cat, Polaris and Yamaha. Unlike Cat it uses a stationary ramp. The rollers move up and down the ramp exerting force. Cat and Polaris are the opposite where the roller is stationary and the weights move, exerting force. The T.R.A. is tuneable with its clicker idea. If you are over-revving turn the clicker downward in the number. If under-revving turn it up in the number. This adjusts RPM in 150-200 RPM increments.

Clutch (Basics)

When the sled is standing still (idling), the drive belt is sitting high in the back clutch and low in the front clutch. As you apply throttle the drive clutch sheaves squeeze the belt causing the belt to rise in the front clutch and drop in the back clutch. The helix degree angle in the back clutch changes upshift and downshift characteristics. The lower helix angle improves downshift. A higher degree improves upshift.

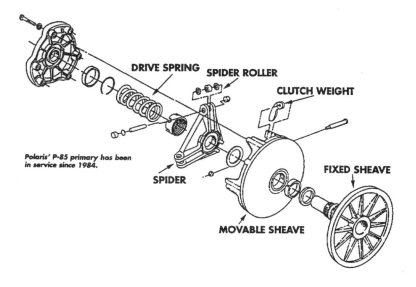

Front Clutch (Courtesy of Polaris)

Clutching (Out of the Box)

Many riders have an unspoken truce between themselves and their OEM clutches. Rider pulls the throttle, clutch makes the sled move, neither messes with the other's business. There are a few, though, who brave the scorn of OEM engineers and tinker with the clutch setup. Others simply buy whole new clutches to suit their needs.

Before you go monkeying around in a perfectly fine clutch system, take a few minutes and learn what you're getting into.

Drive Clutch (Primary)

The crank shaft connects the power created by the engine to the drive clutch, also known as the primary. Your clutch weights, ramp profile and drive clutch spring tension combination determines the engagement RPM of your snowmobile. As the drive clutch rotates, centrifugal force causes the clutch weights to pivot outward, exerting force on the spider arm rollers. As the weights exert more force on the spider rollers, overcoming the force of the drive clutch spring, they push the moveable primary sheave toward the fixed drive sheave. As the engine spins faster, the pulley spins faster, the two sheaves get closer, and the front "gear" gets larger. This is why the drive clutch is said to be RPM sensing.

Driven Pulley (Secondary)

The primary delivers the power from the engine via the belt to the secondary pulley. The idle position on the secondary, or driven pulley is with the sheaves close together, creating a very large "gear". The starting ratio has to be low enough to break a sled loose from a crust of snow and ice.

Once the sled begins movement, the primary sheave begins its travel inward, increasing the front "gear" size. Since the belt does not stretch to accommodate the growing front "gear", it is drawn into the driven sheaves, causing them to move apart from each other, making a smaller rear "gear". The rate at which the secondary opens up to allow the belt to travel inward is controlled by the torque cam, more commonly known as the helix. Once the "gear" ratio hits 1:1, the snowmobile has achieved high gear. This is where your sled tries to maintain operation. Some transmission designs will shift to an "overdrive" ratio of .8 to 1. Overdrive designs allow for lower overall gear ratios at engagement with equal high gear, overall ratios.

However, if the track leaves the hardpack and hits powder, extra resistance is placed on the drive system. This torque forces the sheaves of the secondary to move closer, creating a larger rear "gear" and backshift has occurred. The amount of torque needed to backshift is determined by the amount of spring pressure and angle of the cam in the secondary. The speed and smoothness of the backshift is governed by the angle of the helix. This is why the secondary is said to be torque sensing.

The Helix (Cam)

The helix or cam has three identical angular ramps which determines the rate of upshift and backshift. The cover on the outer hub of the secondary contains three buttons which travel up and down the helix ramps, pushing the movable sheave outward (upshift), or allowing it to move inward (backshift). The steeper the ramp angle, the faster a sled will upshift. If a helix has a very low angle of incline, it will allow faster backshift. The key for a helix designer is to find the perfect balance rapid acceleration and solid backshifting.

BELT PROBLEMS

1. Uneven belt wear on one side only. Check for pulley misalignment. If the pulleys are not aligned, check your manual for alignment procedures and follow the OEM recommendations. If your pulleys are aligned, check for loose engine mounts — you may need to replace or tighten your engine mounts. Another cause might be from gouged or scratched pulley surfaces. If this is the case, have your pulleys ground or polished to remove any deformities.

2. Belt glazed excessively or baked appearance. There can be several reasons for this; 1) Insufficient pressure is being applied to the sides of the belt. If so, check your drive pulley for smooth actuation. 2) You may have excessive oil on the surface of your pulleys.

Check the bearing seals and wipe your pulley surfaces down with a degreasing agent. 3) Another possible cause may be insufficient preload on the driven spring. You will need to consult the Operator's Manual for this remedy. 4) You could also be experiencing excessive operation in low gear position. Inspect your driven pulley for correct

Heat Checked Glazed Belt

operation. If your transmission is calibrated for use with a soft belt, use of a hard belt will result in a glazed, slipping belt. The drive belt is a calibrated part of the transmission system.

3. Excessive top-width wear on belt. If your driver pulley is not actuating smoothly, it can cause excessive belt slippage. This will result in your belt wearing out prematurely. Another cause might be your pulleys. Check the pulleys for any scratches or deformities and repair if needed. Your belt could possibly have the wrong angle. If this appears to the be problem, consult your dealer. It could be you have just worn the belt out and all you have to do is replace your belt with a new one.

4. Belt worn narrow in one section. This symptom is usually caused by excessive slippage in the drive pulley as a result of several different situations. You could have a locked track. If so, try rotating the track by hand until it is free. If that does not seem to be the problem, check your converter for proper operation. It may need to be repaired or replaced. If your engine idle speed is too high, it will result in a narrow spot on your belt. Simply reducing the

Classic case of spin burn caused by a locked track, converter not functioning properly or an engine idle speed which is too high.

idle speed will eliminate this problem. A notch ground into the belt will cause a severe vibration when driving the snowmobile.

5. Belt too tight during engine idle. The first thing you may want to check is whether you have the correct belt on your machine. Make sure the belt you are using is the recommended belt for your sled. If the belt is right, check the center distance between the Primary and Secondary. Make sure the dimension is correct, according to what the manufacturer says. If everything seems to be in order, check the idler bearing, it may have seized. If it has, replace it with a new one.

6. Belt disintegration. Occasionally a belt seems to fly apart. This is usually the result of excessive heat buildup on the belt caused by running the belt at high speeds for extended periods of time. You can avoid this by reducing your engine RPM's at high speeds. Another source of heat buildup is operating in a low gear position for long periods of time—this causes excessive slippage. Check your converter to make sure it is operating properly. Misaligned pulleys can cause the belt to flip over and it will eventually disintegrate. Aligning the pulleys according to the Operator's Manual will prevent this from happening.

7. Belt Edge Cord Broken. Forcing the belt to track in misaligned pulleys will have an adverse effect on the cords. This will result in broken cords and cord pop-out. To reduce the chances of this happening, be sure the driver and driven pulleys are aligned. If your engagement speed is too high, it has a tendency to place an

Cord pop-out is typically caused by pulley misalignment, engagement speed being too high or improper belt installation.

extreme shock load on the cords. Reducing your engagement speed will reduce this problem.

8. Flex Cracks Between Cogs. Flex cracks become predominate when: the belt is worn out; the sled is operated excessively in low gear position; the temperatures are extremely low; or there is a bent pulley flange causing belt flutter. If the belt is worn out, simply replace it. Excessive operation in the low gear position may be caused by faulty converter. Check the converter to be sure it is operating properly. If it is so cold that your eyelids freeze shut, then your belt is probably too cold. Try warming it up slowly. If the belt is flapping around, check the pulleys for any kind of damage and, if need be, repair or replace them.

9. Broken belt. Shock loading on the belt can sometimes cause the belt to break. Shock loading can be caused by: the engagement RPM being too high; the belt hanging up on the bottom of the driven pulley; or maybe the track is locked up. You can remedy these situations by either reducing the engagement RPM, replacing the belt (because it is too short), or rotating the track by hand until it is free.

A little preventative maintenance on your part can give you a lot of enjoyable riding.

By doing simple maintenance on your drive belts, you will get the most from your sled.

This is a classic case of sheared cogs resulting from inproper belt installation, the belt rubbing a stationary object or a seized idler bearing.

Flex Cracks between cogs are the result of considerable use, excessive operation in low gear or extremely low temperatures.

Removing and Installing Drive Clutch

Engine Crank Shaft

Jack Shaft

Tools needed: clutch puller, breaker bar, socket set, torque wrench. When reinstalling torque to manufacturers specs.

Chapter 9

TRACKS, SKID FRAME, LIMITER STRAP

Tracks are an important component for your type of riding. Since tracks vary in lug depth and are available in short and long track models, your choice is critical for your type of riding. Knowing what to do with a skid frame and limiter strap helps you get the edge.

Track Lugs

Lug height ranges from .75" to 2" deep lugs designed for your riding needs.

Trail Tracks

A shallow lug such as .75", .92" and 1" is preferred for trail riding

Powder Trail (Versatility)

In this snow condition a 1.25" lug is used as a dual purpose on or off the trail

Powder Specialized Track

The 2" deep lug is very popular with mountain riders and is recommended for deep snow. Some vibration could be felt on a hard packed trail.

Greasing the Skid Frame

The moving parts of the skid frame should be greased as regular maintenance. Greasing the skid frame and suspension reduces friction and keeps moisture out of the bushings, bearings, etc. Check idler wheels for loose side play and replace if bearings are worn. Spraying WD-40 on after a ride works well. Use low temperature grease.

Track Tension

With the sled up by the back bumper track tension should be between 3/4" and 1 1/4". If too loose, track can ratchet. Loosen rear idler wheel bolts before adjusting.

Tracks, Drive Chain (Overtightened)

Overtightening your snowmobile track can cause premature hifax wear and place added stress on the track and driveline components.

On the drive chain in a snowmobile chaincase, overtightened chains accelerate wear on chain, sprockets and driveline bearings. With overtightening tracks and chains, a reduction in usable power will result

Track Alignment

Take a look at the distance between rails and track clips. They should be even. If not, tighten the wide side (near the rear idler wheel). Loosen rear idler wheel bolts before adjusting. Tighten idler bolts.

Limiter Strap (Stopper Strap)

This is located at the front of the skid frame. Sleds may have either one or two. Attached to the skid, it looks like a black nylon belt and limits the amount of travel of the front of skid frame.

Locating the Limiter Strap

Some sleds have a turn-
ing knob to lengthen or
shorten straps. Some
are nut and bolt type
and another is a knob
up near the handlebars
which eliminates the
need to get your hands
under the sled at the
front of the skid frame.

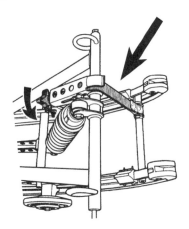

A Must Know

Adjusting your limiter strap is a must and something you should learn. Getting to know what this
little device does, ensures against lost performance.

Shortening Strap (Trail Riding)

When you shorten or tighten the limiter strap it
pulls the front of the skid up towards the tunnel
taking weight off front of track. This adds ski pressure, gives less track footprint and is used for
better handling on the trail.

Snowmobile
Front

Lengthening Strap (Deep Snow & Mountain Riding)

Lengthen the strap for deep snow and mountain riding. This puts more track footprint on the snow.

Flat

Pivoting

Too much shock and spring pressure on front of the rear suspension can cause pivoting. To correct this, tighten limiter straps and loosen spring on front of rear suspension.

Pivots here

Hyfax Care

Attached to the underside of the skid rails the track (track clips) ride on this polyethylene type of plastic. When it wears down there is a danger of metal to metal contact and track damage. Keep an eye on these and replace if suspecting they are worn out. They are inexpensive and offer good insurance against track and clip damage. Use ice scratchers in low snow condition.

THE TUNNEL

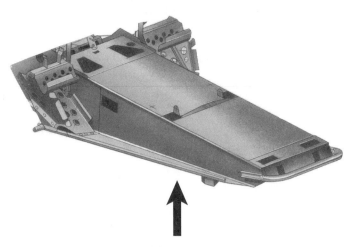

Rear Suspension
Fits in Tunnel

REAR SUSPENSION

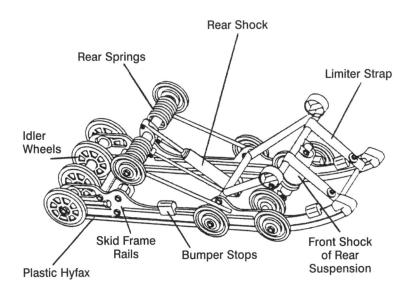

Rear Shock

Rear Springs

Limiter Strap

Idler
Wheels

Skid Frame
Rails

Bumper Stops

Front Shock
of Rear
Suspension

Plastic Hyfax

Drivers

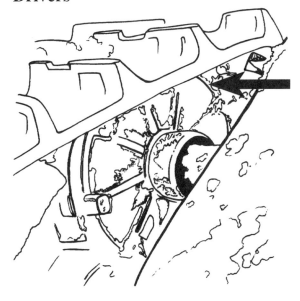

Drivers fit
on drive
axle and
drives the
track.

Chapter 10

SKIS

The ski type and adjustment make a significant difference for your particular riding style.

Type of Ski

You can choose between metal and plastic construction. Metal tends to stick more on the snow and is usually heavier. Plastic is easier to turn and has less friction.

Width

Standard width is 5 and 1/2 inches, but can range up to 7 and 1/2 inches. The wider the ski the more effort it takes to turn in powder snow. The 6 inch width may offer the best balance of floatation and good carving. There is also a bolt on skin10" wide.

Rocker Keel Skis

The bottom of the ski is designed like a rocker, the rocker point sitting below the spindle. This design can make for easier steering.

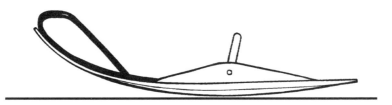

Rocker

Ski Weight

Skis range from approximately 12 pounds a pair to 26 pounds. A real weight saving is possible here.

Mountain Skis

When you get off the trail you need a good carving ski to keep control, pick your line and stay on it. This is where multi-keel gets attention. They add control when side-hilling and can keep your sled holding on a slope. (See page 141, Side Bar Skis)

10%. The percentage of present snowmobile owners who buy a new sled each year.

Various Keel Designs

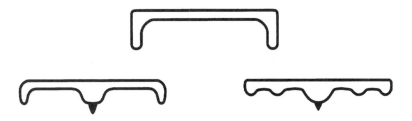

Multiple Keels

The after marketers now have skis ranging from one to five keels. Claims are made that these designs eliminate darting, and offer better control. They can be better than stock skis.

Colors

You can really dress up your sled with a variety of ski colors. Some manufacturers offer as many as seven colors.

Carbides

The more carbides that contact the surface the more aggressive the bite on hard surfaces. Carbide ranges from 4 - 10 inches per wear bar. Carbide exposure means little in powder snow.

Ski-Loops

Bright color on the ski-loops allows you to see your ski tips. This is really a directional help on the trail, in the trees, or picking a course going up or down a hill. Grab and tug on ski-loops to aid in getting your sled unstuck.

Trail Skis

Trail skis are designed usually with one keel in the centre approximately 5 and 1/4 inches ski width and carbides from 4 inches long to 10 inches long for a desired trail bite.

Chapter 11

TROUBLESHOOTING

If your sled becomes immobile in the back country or on the trail, these tips can help save your day and a towing job.

Engine Will Not Start (1 through 13)

(1) Make certain there is gas in the tank, fuel line, and the fuel lever is on.

Ignition

(2) Be sure the key is on, the emergency stop button is up, the tether cord is attached, and plug wires connected.

Fuel

(3) Make sure fuel line is not clogged. You can pull fuel line off and check for free flow. To check filter, remove it and blow through it. To see if fuel is flowing at all, disconnect it at the carb end, and pull starter rope. If still no fuel in line, the gas tank filter may be plugged.

Choke or Primer

(4) A cold engine requires a richer mixture than normal to start. Carbureted snowmobile engines are equipped with chokes, enrichers and/or primers for cold starting. A primer is a manual fuel pump that allows you to pump raw fuel into the intake. Two to three full pumps of the primer are generally needed. Hold the throttle partially open when cranking till the engine fires. Additional pumping of the primer may be required till the engine gains some heat.

Some carburetors are equipped with a choke plate in the carburetor bore. The choke should be closed and the throttle held open when cranking. When engine fires, release the throttle and disengage the choke as the engine gains heat.

Carburetors such as the Mikuni have a separate enriching circuit. It is sometimes called a choke but must be used differently than a real choke plate. Engage the "choke" for starting but do not open the throttle while cranking. Opening the throttle will allow air to bypass the enriching circuit. Allow the engine to gain some heat before disengaging the "choke".

Air Box

(5) If engine is still not starting, try a direct primer by removing the air box and pouring a small capful of gas into the rear carb throat, or in to spark plug hole.

Flooded Engine

(6) Shut gas off. Remove spark plugs and dry them out if they are wet with gas. Pull over engine more than five or ten times with plugs removed. Be sure to turn off ignition. Turn ignition on. See if plugs spark and then install them and try starting. Hold throttle wide open till engine fires.

Temporary Air Box Removal (Hard Starting)

(7) Remove air box to see if engine will start. This gives more air to carb. Do not run engine continuously with the box removed or engine could seize. Once the engine starts replace the air box immediately.

Hot or Flooded

(8) Depress throttle lever by one half throttle while pulling starter rope. This adds air to the combustion chambers.

Float Bowl Drain

(9) Drain carb float bowl. If this starts engine, it was probably flooded.

Dry Lines/Dry Plugs

(10) Remove spark plugs and check for lack of fuel. If plugs are dry it can mean clogged carb passages, clogged fuel line, or air lock. Tap on float bowl, bottom of carb. Stuck floats or a faulty fuel pump may be the cause of the problem.

Spark Check

(11) Remove plugs and lay them on the cylinder head with plug wires connected. Pull starter rope. Plugs should spark blue color. If no spark, check tether, kill switch, and key. You can try new plugs if all else checks out. Check spark plug caps. Check your plugs with another machine. Plug wires leading back to the coil should be checked.

High Altitude Kit.

(12) If starting troubles occur at a high elevation make sure you have the right kit installed. Hard starting can be due to the wrong sized pilots in the kit you have.

Sea Level Kit

(13) Be sure you have sea level kit installed if most riding is done below 4,000 feet, otherwise hard starting can occur.

Clunking Noises

Jerking motion and noises during slow acceleration can be caused by wrong belt length, width or excessive wear. Wearing out jackshaft bearings or speedo side bearings may also be a cause.

Ratcheting

The track being too loose or misaligned, can cause ratcheting, also, it can relate to the chain case when the chain is not properly adjusted, usually too loose.

High Pitch Zing Sound

This noise can indicate the drive belt is worn out or clutches are hot. Let them cool down and install a correct belt, preferably a new one.

Engine Running But Sled Won't Move

This can be caused by any of the following: clutches too hot, belt slipping, snow and ice in suspension clogging up drivers axle, no drive belt on, or track frozen to ground. More serious causes include broken drive axle; jack shaft, or broken chain in chaincase.

Temperature Light On (Over Heated)

Stop. Check for coolant leaks. Low snow conditions causes overheating. Running snow ice scratchers are helpful.

Air Cooled Engine Overheating

Shut off the machine and let it cool with the hood open. Check fan belt condition and tension.

Engine Bogs.

Water in fuel.	Idle too low.
Wrong drive belt.	Improper altitude kit
Jetting too rich.	Jetting too lean.
Restricted fuel.	Too low clutch engagement.
Out of time.	Dead plug.

Cool Cylinder (Dead Plug)

If your engine is running rough with big loss of power, stop and carefully touch each exhaust pipe. The pipe that is cool probably has a dead plug. If you don't want to touch the pipe, put a bit of snow on the pipe. If it doesn't melt, that plug could be dead.

Poor Idling

- Plugged pilots in carb.
- Wrong pilot size.
- Incorrect idle screw setting.
- Incorrect air screw setting.
- Water in fuel.
- Intake air leak.
- Choke is on.
- Arcing plug wires.
- One dead cylinder.
- Worn idle screws or slides.

Setting the idle (engine off) Mikuni Carbs.

Remove air box from carbs. Get a view of carb slides. Unscrew idle screws counterclockwise until they no longer touch the slide. Turn idle screw clockwise until the screw just touches the slide. Do with all carbs. Turn in 2 turns. This is a good starting point to set the desired idle. For air screw setting generally turn clockwise until screw stops, then back out 1.5 turns. Check synchronization of slides before reinstalling airbox. Reinstall air box. Normal idle is about 1800 to 2500 RPM.

Sled Goes Ahead by Itself

It could be wrong belt installed for that sled or improper belt deflection adjustment. Be sure you can read the letters on the belt for proper installation when looking from the clutch side of the sled.

Vibration Causes

Deep lug track design, clutches out of balance, a motor crankshaft twisted, too rich jetting in carbs, worn or loose motor mounts, drive axle bent, jack shaft bearings. Drivers are not true on a drive axle. Flat spot on idler wheel, broken track lugs. Check for broken or loose engine mounts. A drive belt with a notch worn into it from the clutch will also cause a nasty vibration.

Clutch Bog

Too low clutch engagement. Try stiffer drive clutch spring to increase engagement. Increase driven pulley sheave pressure. Worn drive belt, gearing too high for altitude, or broken motor mount.

Chapter 12

SAFETY & TRAIL MANNERS

Snowmobiling is a sport that requires experience, skill, and knowledge of how to behave on the snow trails. There are traditions and a code of conduct that should be learned and respected by all participants.

The toll of injuries and death are usually needless and always tragic. Misbehavior of a few is threatening to bring in more legislation. This usually means more restrictions, fees and patrol costs. So it is in the interest of all sledders to take the code seriously and make the sport safer and more enjoyable.

Don't Take Chances

Take maps along of areas you are going to ride in.

Preparedness

Plan your trip and bring all the necessary items for the day's adventure.

Weather Conditions

Weather in the hills may not be like that at home. If there is a settlement or a mountain lodge in the vicinity, a phone call may be wise if forecasts are not definite.

Snow Blindness

Use UV protection sunglasses and/or tinted face shield on your helmet. High definition (yellow) lenses make the landscape seem clear and depth perception better.

Protecting Environment

Snowmobilers are usually good environmentalists because they love the purity of the fresh outdoors and unspoiled scenery. Some trails are cleared and maintained by snowmobile clubs. Avoid hitting young trees and shrubs and of course, never leave litter behind.

Night Riding

Many snowmobile accidents occur after dark. If you ride at night here are a few hints: illuminate your sled, use halogen headlight and high beam whenever possible, flash your brake light and keep snow off it, put reflective tape on your sled and on the back of your suit and helmet.

Fences and Wires

Stay well away from fences. Snow drifts cover them and hide extreme danger. We have all heard what happens when a sledders body hits a wire fence. Be careful near telephone polls because the guy wires can decapitate a rider.

Survival Preparedness

A survival course or a little reading up on the subject is important. Look into a global positioning system if you are a real distance sledder. Remember to bring the items listed in the survival kit.

Lake Riding (Not Recommended)

Be very careful. Sledders are lost to this fate every season.

WARNING:
IF YOU DON'T KNOW . . . DON'T GO!

If you encounter slush and soft spots and feel your sled sinking, keep it moving, since a sled with speed has a relatively light footprint.

Approved CCSO snowmobiling hand signals.

RIGHT TURN

Left arm raised at shoulder height, elbow bent and forearm vertical with palm of hand flat..

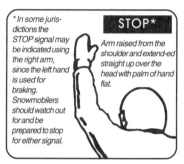

STOP*

* In some jurisdictions the STOP signal may be indicated using the right arm, since the left hand is used for braking. Snowmobilers should watch out for and be prepared to stop for either signal.

Arm raised from the shoulder and extend-ed straight up over the head with palm of hand flat.

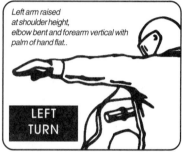

LEFT TURN

Left arm raised at shoulder height, elbow bent and forearm vertical with palm of hand flat..

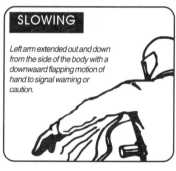

SLOWING

Left arm extended out and down from the side of the body with a downwaard flapping motion of hand to signal warning or caution.

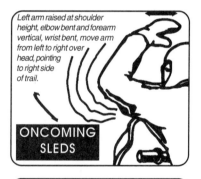

ONCOMING SLEDS

Left arm raised at shoulder height, elbow bent and forearm vertical, wrist bent, move arm from left to right over head, pointing to right side of trail.

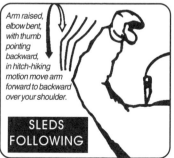

SLEDS FOLLOWING

Arm raised, elbow bent, with thumb pointing backward, in hitch-hiking motion move arm forward to backward over your shoulder.

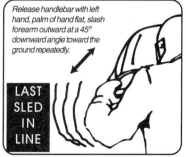

LAST SLED IN LINE

Release handlebar with left hand, palm of hand flat, slash forearm outward at a 45° downward angle toward the ground repeatedly.

Safety Regulations

1. A snowmobile may not be operated within 7.5m (approx. 25 ft.) of the travelled portion of a high way except to cross the highway or when necessary for loading and unloading purposes.
2. Before crossing a public road, stop, look and listen. If the way is clear, it is safe to cross.
3. Snowmobiles must be equipped with lights, and it is recommended that they be turned on during daytime travel.
4. Always drive on the right hand side of the trail.
5. Any person who drives or is a passenger of a snowmobile must wear an approved helmet, securely fastened.
6. Obey all signs posted along the trails.
7. Snowmobiling while under the influence of alchohol or drugs is strictly prohibited by law.
8. Always travel in the company of other snowmobilers.
9. Dress appropriately for the conditions, be adequately protected from the cold.
10. Permission has been granted for the use of trails only. If you leave the trails you may be trespassing.

Avoid wearing long or loose scarves, shoelaces, etc., which could get caught in moving parts of a snowmobile.

Insulated Float Coat

The Insulated
Float Coat
is a floatation-capable
snowsuit which will
keep you warm in cold
weather or in cold
water. It performs much
like a wet suit does.
Wiggie's Inc.,
of Grand Junction, Colorado
is a company which
can supply this.

If you ever fall through the ice, this floatation suit
could give you enough time to save your life. Suits
are also offered by some snowmobile manufacturers.

2.2 Million. The approximate number of registered
snowmobilers in North America.

Code of Ethics

1. I will be a good sportsman and conservationist. I recognize that people will judge all snowmobilers by my actions. I will use my influence with other snowmobile owners and operators to promote sportsmanlike conduct.

2. I will not litter any trails or areas, nor will I pollute streams or lakes. I will carry out what I carry in.

3. I will not damage living trees, shrubs or other natural features.

4. I will respect other people's properties and rights.

5. I will lend a helping hand when I see someone in need.

6. I will make myself and my vehicle available to assist in search and rescue operations.

7. I will not interfere with the activities of other winter sportsmen. I will respect their right to enjoy their recreational activity.

8. I will know and obey all federal, state or provincial and local rules regulating the operation of snowmobiles in area where I use my vehicle.

9. I will not harass wildlife.

10. I will not snowmobile where prohibited.

Chapter 13
DO'S & DON'TS

If you fail to abide by the rules when sledding someone will eventually flag you down and let you know about it.

Be Courteous

Keeping good relations with cross country skiers and others using the outdoors is important. Stopping for a few friendly words may be all it takes.

Knowledge

Do pass on knowledge of the sport. It can help others in trouble and also enhances the sport.

Private Land

Ask permission to sled on private property. It can lead to trouble if you don't. It also puts a negative image on snowmobilers.

Helping Others

Give a hand when you see another one broken down or stuck. It is almost certain that you will need help someday.

Planning

Have all your gear together the day before you ride. Get a good night's sleep and be ready to pull out early for the day ahead.

Respect

Do respect all wildlife and the sensitive alpine areas protecting the beauty of nature.

Railway Tracks

Do not ride on railway tracks. Trains always win.

Ice

Check the cracks out there and ask others, especially any available experts, for advice about the safety situation. Watch for creek mouths where normal looking snow can conceal the underlying ice thinned by the warmer flowing water. In moderate climates where temperatures alternate around the freezing level, it may be a sound policy to stay off lakes and rivers.

Trail Debris

Remember the chunks of dirt and ice that are thrown off your track. Think of those you are passing when the ice chunks fly.

Trail Hills

Don't pass going up a hill and risk a head on collision. Don't pass or stop your sled on a corner.

Storms

If it is rainy and stormy going in, don't push on. Just turn your sled around and go back to the truck. If you get caught in a white-out, be prepared to wait it out until things clear up, unless you're very familiar with the terrain.

Alcohol and Litter

Chemically, alcohol reduces body temperature. Littering will get the environmentalists turning you in and whole areas will be closed to snowmobilers.

Coming Back

Don't get caught in the dark. Turn for home when there are still two or three hours of daylight left. Getting lost in the wilderness dark is a scary experience.

Frozen Track

Don't engage the clutch when the track is frozen to the ground. Your belt will last about two seconds. Jack up sled at the end of the day's ride. Bounce suspension on cold days to remove ice and snow.

Cold Seizure

Let your engine warm up for a few minutes. Cold seizure happens when riding starts before engine reaches operating temperature.

Clutch Starting (Caution)

Don't turn or play with drive clutch when the switch is on. The engine may start and cause injury.

Sled Surrender

Don't drive your sled into a bowl filled with 3 to 4 feet of fresh powder. You might not be able to climb out. Not even a tow sled can pull you out. A helicopter can cost the price of the sled to recover it. Walking twenty miles out can be a disaster and if it snows overnight you have the problem of locating your machine.

Chapter 14
AVALANCHES

One of the main motivations for writing this handbook was the increasing number of snowmobilers killed by avalanches every year. Here are some tips to escape that fate and avoid becoming avalanche bait.
Also learn about avalanches by reading and/or attending an avalanche course or awareness lecture.

Causes

A change in weather conditions like a sudden rise in temperature, the weight of your machine and the echoing noise of the sleds can pull the trigger on a snowslide.

Beacons

Carry the locator beacon on your person and not attached to the sled. They must be turned on before riding starts, all of them. Do a trial of finding another person by having them hide while the others seek. The cost is about two to three hundred dollars. Don't do the trial in avalanche areas.

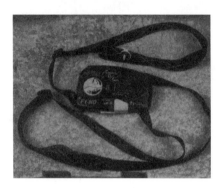

Slope Steepness

Learn to recognize avalanche terrain. Most victims are caught on slope inclines of 25 to 60 degrees.

Winter/Spring

During winter the north facing, sun shaded slopes are cold and tend to be unstable. In the spring as it warms up, the slopes facing south are more unstable.

Safe Riding

Stay away from steep terrain known as an avalanche path from previous slides. Ride on ridge tops or in heavily wooded areas as much as possible. Always make sure your path is sprinkled with some type of vegitation. Do not ride up or in the centre of a slope.

Snowmobile (Stuck On A Slope)

If a person gets stuck on a slope, do not go to help dig out the sled Let him work on it by himself. The theory is that if an avalanche hits, more people will be caught. If you stand and watch and an avalanche does occur, you will be able to go to the rescue and dig him out. Adding more people to a slope simply increases the stress on that slope and increases the possibility of an avalanche being triggered. There are a number of cases where one or more people were killed as the second person came up to help a stuck rider and the weight of both riders triggered the avalanche. Finally, while your buddy is up on the slope, all others should position themselves off to the side of the bottom of the slope so that they are not in danger if the slope releases. The point is that if an avalanche occurs you only want one person caught, thereby reducing the number of victims and greatly improving your odds of successfully rescuing him.

New Snow

The danger increases with a substantial, freshly deposited snowfall. This heavy load of new snow slides off previously frozen crust. Call avalanche info center.

Crossing Danger Zones

When crossing danger zones, riders go one at a time, avoiding the bottom of the slope. Instead, ride up the edges close to the trees.

Escaping

If it happens to you, ride to the side of the rolling snow. This is the shortest distance to safety. If knocked off your sled swim like body surfing at the ocean. When under the snow try to make an air cave around your face to give you some extra minutes of air. You must fight to survive.

Time of the Year

Avalanches occur from the beginning of winter to the end. Call an information centre for advisories.

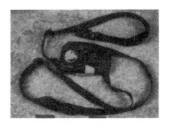

Beacons

Probes

Shovels

Take these along when sledding in avalanche terrain.

Chapter 15

SURVIVAL IN THE BACK COUNTRY

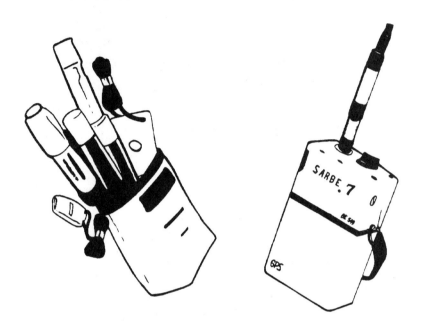

Any trip into winter wilderness can run into unexpected emergencies. It pays to know survival basics, expecially in situations of getting separated from the group, becoming lost or caught in a white-out.

Global Positioning System

Get a ground to air satelite transitter with long lasting batteries. Take spare batteries to make sure. GPS stands for the satelite based Global Positioning System. This is something designed and installed by the U.S. Department of Defense that can be used by all of us. It tells exactly where you are, in relation to where you have been, or would like to be. All you have to do is buy a receiver, learn how to use it, and it's almost impossible to stay lost from that day forward. For a snowmobiler all you have to do is punch a button when you leave your starting point. No matter how many turns you make or how many different directions you have dedcided to go, your GPS receiver will tell you exactly how far away (in a direct line) from your starting point you are, and what direction you have to take to get back.

Distress Signal

Buy the floating type of signal. When launched the flares can be seen from a distance of 15 to 20 miles. Outdoor stores should have them.

Groups

Being in a larger group is the most helpful for survival. Safety in numbers applies here.

Food supplies

Estimate the duration of your emergency situation and the total supply of food and water. Eat and drink enough to ward off panic, but also ration according to your time estimate.

Fire

Of primary importance is staying warm. Start gathering dry or dead wood, and get a good fire burning. In daylight throw on some green branches for a smoke signal.

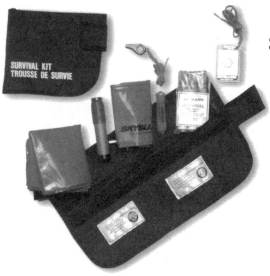

Survival kit

Survival Kit

Always carry a First Aid Kit. The following are some basic items for a trip of some distance:

- space blankets
- nylon cord
- compass
- signal mirror
- candles
- leather man tool
- light weight folding shovel
- duct tape
- maps of area
- flashlight, extra batteries
- waterproof matches
- high energy dehydrated food

- water
- two-man tent
- aspirins
- safety pins
- salt
- wire type saw
- beef jerky
- axe
- plastic tarp
- bandages
- aluminum foil
- small diameter wire
- sugar cubes
- granola bars (lots)
- separate emergency kit
- tin can to boil water
- hunting licence & small rifle for game

Space Blankets

Sew the space blankets together at home for sleeping bag type protection.

Bad Situation

If something does occur and it is impractical or impossible to backtrack, stay together. Handle a bad situation by remaining calm, dry and warm, and decide on a plan. Knowing how to use your survival tools can ease a big chunk of anxiety at a time like this.

Shelter

Find a place out of the wind, away from steep slopes, preferably facing south. If snow is 2 to 4 feet deep, you can dig a 10 by 10 foot square hole and put a tarp over it, using tree branches for support. Use tree branches to cover if you don't have a tarp.

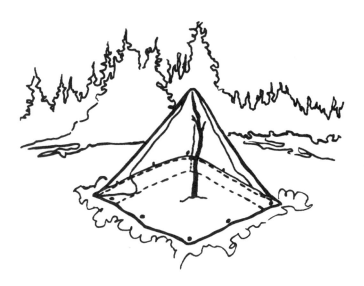

Ground Distress Signals

When you lay out the signals make them as large as possible. Use ashes, rocks, branches, anything dark to outline the signal. On a sunny day use a mirror or other reflecting material to alert rescuers.

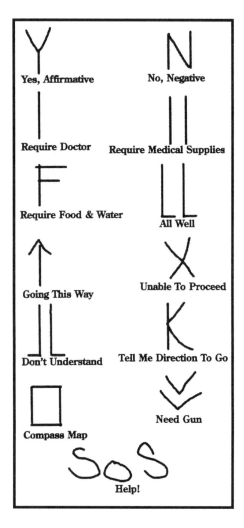

Cell Phone

Many people have been rescued due to this modern miracle. Be sure to take extra new batteries along. Remember, rescue attempts stop when it becomes dark. Don't let the phone get wet.

Fast Moving Clouds

If you see fast moving clouds coming towards you, get back on the trail fast. You only have approximately 5 to 10 minutes before a white-out or storm can hit. Don't ride in a white out. Find shelter and wait till storm passes.

Water

Melt snow with a fire instead of in your mouth. Boil it if you can and this will kill the bacteria in the snow.

Knowing Which Direction

The moon and sun come up in the east, and set in the west. Hemlock and pine tree tops lean eastward.

Don't Fall Asleep

Take turns sleeping. Have your partner stay awake and wake you at intervals. Extreme cold can put you in deep sleep and kill.

Big Smoke

Build a fire in daylight and use wet wood and boughs. Take oil from your sled and put on fire.

Fire Wall

If you can find a rock wall, build a fire next to it. The heat will reflect back to you.

Two-Man Tent

When travelling into backcountry 25 to 50 miles, consider taking a compact two-man tent. If you use it be sure to leave an air vent, to avoid suffocation.

Tree Squirrel Snare

Use limp line or limp wire.

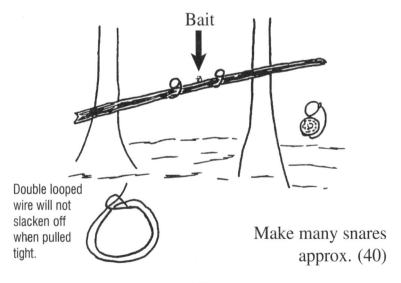

Bait

Double looped wire will not slacken off when pulled tight.

Make many snares approx. (40)

Snow Gathered Mound Cave

Under low snow conditions, gather snow into a mound with diameter about 10 feet and height about 4 to 5 feet. Before digging out entrance let the snow mound set for about 1/2 to 1 hour. You can use the sled's windshield for a shovel. Remember, don't make it airtight.

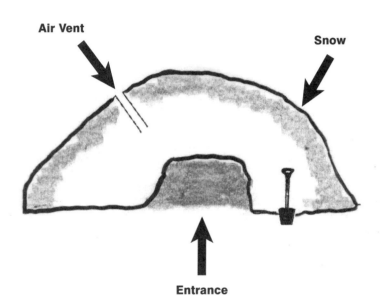

Emergency Winter Food

Inner bark of pine, poplar, birch or willow can be eaten fresh, brewed into tea, cut into strips and cooked like noodles or dried and ground into flour. Pine seeds can also be eaten.

Snow Cave

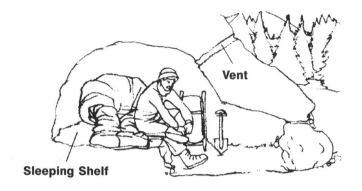

Vent

Sleeping Shelf

Snow cave resembles an igloo, but instead of being built of blocks, it is scooped out of a snowbank. Design shown has a rear sleeping shelf. Another style has a central cooking area with two-person sleeping shelves on each side. The roof should be at least 2 feet thick with a sloping venthole. Check the venthole before cooking to make sure it is clear of snow. The preferred site for snow cave is in deep snow. A lot of digging is necessary, so snow shovels are a must.

1 in 5 snowmobilers have taken an organized snow-mobile safety course.

Chapter 16
MISCELLANEOUS TIPS

Shop Dolly

A circle of five dolly wheels instead of the usual three or four gets better results when moving your sled in the shop.

Bumper Jack

A Chevrolet type bumper jack. Weld the bottom plate stand to the jack. Put a pin in the post to stop the mechanism from slipping to the bottom.

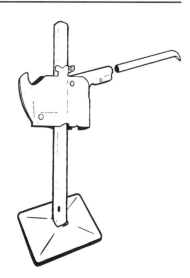

Snow Flap Holder

Use a metal S shape flap holder. Insert S hooks into the flap, pull up, and hang on the bumper. Much needed for backing up. Be sure to remove S hooks when riding since it can get caught and tear the track.

S-Hook

Longer Bumper

Put on an extended back bumper approximately six inches longer than stock. The leverage for lifting increases greatly and helps save your back. Great for stuck conditions.

Cross Over Sled Lift

To get a sled on its side, grab a ski loop and pull up and across to other ski.

Clunk! Clunk! Clunk!

If you hear this at lower speeds, most likely it is the wrong belt. It could also be wrong length, wrong width, or belt has burned a flat spot.

Side Bar Skis

For more control on your skis, try mounting side bars on the under der side as shown in illustration.
Get the 3/8" 7/16" dia. wear bars without carbides at your dealer. Great for mountains.

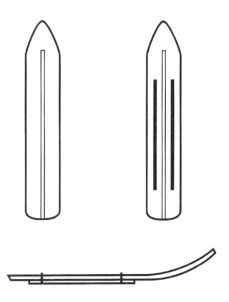

Gas Cans

Fill gas can as full as you can. This stops any sloshing of gas and any build up of fumes in the air space of can.

Still Camera

Take a small camera and put it in your fanny bag. Try to take pictures with a lot of contrast and sunshine. Do not forget, snow can fool a camera.

Fanny Bag

This straps to your handle bars and has enough room for a small camera, altimeter, sunglasses, a small clock, and compass.

Fun Factor

This is a sled that has quick reflexes and a light feel even though it might not be light. These sleds are fun to ride, and usually personalized to the rider's wants.

Helmet Cam Holder

Keep your hands free. Trying to ride a snowmobile and taking video is not only dangerous, but very difficult. A neat little invention to keep your hands free is a camera clamp. This video camera holder clamps to the side of your helmet. They are advertised in snowmobile magazines.

Mirror

When you cannot see under your engine, carburettor, etc., use a mirror.

Water Eliminator

This attaches to the end of the fuel gauge and is left in the tank for six weeks. Remember, water in the fuel means trouble.

Tippiness

If you have dropped the skid out of the tunnel and now experience some tippiness which is not acceptable, put skid back in stock holes.

Dolly Under Skis

To put the dolly under skis, grab the ski loop and pull straight up. This lifts it enough to let the dolly under and not hurt your back. For lifting back of sled use a bumper jack or sled lifting device.

Non-Spill Funnel

The design of this fun-
nel greatly reduces gas
spillage.

Tachometer Tip

Twist tach so maxi-
mum horsepower reads
straight up. Put a thin
width of colored tape on maximum horsepower
RPM reading.

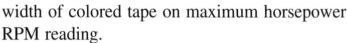

Gas Spilling

To put gas into the tank easily, straddle the sled.
Put both feet on the running boards, like you are
riding standing up.

Broken Clutch

Rare but true. Internal springs and helixes do
break. Having these spare parts, with you could
save a towing job.

Hood Vents In Deep Powder Snow

Block off hood vents to keep snow out of carbs,
and engine. Duct tape will work well.

Studded Track

Be sure there is enough clearance in the tunnel. The studs can gouge holes in the heat exchanger and coolant will spill out.

Exploding Track

Tracks have been known to explode, laying themselves out flat on lake or trail. Check your track for large cracks.

Summer Storage (1 through 7)

(1) Use a fuel stabilizer, running it through the system before shutting down. Fuel starts to lose its freshness after forty five days. Another method is to drain the system by running it dry with the stabilizer added. Drain carbs, fuel lines and gas tank. Many burn downs start in the carbs. They are caused by varnish build up formed by old gas.

Sled (Track)

(2) Keep the track off the floor in storage by having jack under bumper, or 2x4 on edge between lugs, crossways.

Piston Storage Oil

(3) Pour 1 oz. 30 weight oil into spark plug hole, pull starter rope eight or ten times and reinstall spark plugs.

Track & Belts

(4) Remove the belts until snow flies again. Tracks can shrink if loosened. Leave tight!

Fuel Stabilizer

(5) If your fuel system has been drained, or fuel stabilizer such as Sta-Bil added and the engine fogged, it should not be run in the summer.

Oil Spray

(6) With sled on its side, spray your rear suspension with spray lubricant such as WD-40. Go over the whole sled and spray linkages, moving parts, etc.

Plug Exhaust

(7) Plug exhaust and air boxes so bugs and mice can't get in. Put a few moth balls under the hood, but not in the engine or gas tank. Mouse urine can ruin an engine.

Towing

When towing, remove the drive belt of the sled you are towing. Get towed sled close to the bumper of towing sled. Put tow rope on bumper or spindles, not ski loops.

Chapter 17
THE
SNOWMOBILE CLUB

REASONS TO JOIN A CLUB

Hidden Heroes (Volunteers)

These people do the grunt work, clearing brush, grooming trails, organizing events, and keeping members informed of upcoming activities, new riding areas, and places to avoid.

Fees

The fee is $15.00 to $50.00 to join a club in which funds go toward keeping up the trails and paying the maintenance costs of groomer machines, and sport activities.

Safety

Statistics have shown that club members have lower accident rates, since they stress safety conscientious safe riding.

Socializing (Club Sno-a-rama)

These are destination gatherings with people who love the sport as much as you do. At the Sno-a-rama site you will enjoy a roaring campfire, hot coffee and various hot, wholesome foods to warm you. There is something about being in the great outdoors, that can give you a feeling of well being, and the food tastes extra good.

Trail Grooming

Club members who work the groomers, are usually not paid. Members put up sno-mo signs to keep you informed of what's ahead as well as directional information.

Search and Rescue

The authorities may call the local snowmobile clubs for assistance when there is a snow storm. These club members will search for lost people in snow bound vehicles and deliver supplies to the elderly or other shut-ins, helping in any way they can. Lives have been saved, thanks to these very helpful club members. They should be commended for their consideration to those in need.

THE END

GLOSSARY

If you have ever read a snowmobile magazine and find words in there that get you wondering such as: bump steer, scrub, and others, this glossary will be a real help when conversing with other sledders.

Air Box
- Carbs suck air from here, usually through a foam filter to keep snow out.

Alignment
- Refers to skis, clutch, track, using one part to line up exactly with another.

Alpine
- Beautiful open areas above tree growth,

Altitude
- Height above sea level.

Altitude Compensators
- Attached to carb. Automatically adjusts fuel/air mixture for altitude.

Back Shift
- Both pulleys shift to a lower gear ratio.

Base Snow
- Snow that has had time to settle to really firm consistency.

Bogging
- Sluggish acceleration, not crisp.

Boondocker
- Sledder who loves riding in the trees and tight canyons.

Bottoming
- Shocks reaching the end of their travel.

Bowl
- Valley shaped like a salad bowl.

Bump Steer
- Ski toe in or out as front suspension goes through its travel.

Carbides
- Under skis for control.

Center of Gravity
- Center of a mass in uniform gravitational pull.

Chainsaw (Hill Climb)
- Straight up a hill and over the top.

Chemical Warmers
- Man made chemical packets. Produces heat when shaken.

Cinches
- Belt type fabric pulled tight to hold sled down tight when transporting.

Competition Hill Climb.
- Compete on a gruelling uphill course for fastest time.

Converter
- Back clutch.

Cornice
- Wind shaped. Over-hanging snow usually on a steep mountain.

Darting
- Weaving back and forth down a trail.

Deep Lug
- Tracks that have from 1.25" to 2" lug height.

Drive Chain
- Connects jack shaft to drive axle.

Drive Pulley
- Controls engine speed. Transfers power to driven clutch.

Driven Pulley

- Mounts to jack shaft. Receives power through drive belt from drive clutch.

Drivers

- Mounted on a drive axle and used to turn track.

Dyno

- Registers horsepower and torque.

Engagement

- The point at which the engine speed is high enough to move the sled and driver forward.

Fan Cooled

- Engine cooled by air.

Finger Walking

- Sled creeps ahead on its own momentum at top speed.

Fish Scale

- Reads poundage for various settings, such as back clutch tension, track tension, etc.

Fishtailing

- Back of sled sways.

Flex Ski

- Great flexing quality in front half of skis.

Free Horsepower

- Friction reduced sled.

Gas Rack

- Holds gas can securely on sled.

Gun Drilled

- Hollow axle or shaft.

Heat Exchangers

- Attached to inside of the tunnel, snow hits these and aids in cooling the engine.

Helix
- In the driven pulley. Varying degrees change up shift and back shift characteristics.

Heart Stopper.
- A term to describe a very steep hill climb.

High Altitude Kit.
- Installed to reclaim some power loss as one climbs to higher elevations.

High Marking
- Highest snowmobile mark on challenging hills.

Hooker Handles
- Attaches to end of handlebars and aids in controlled turning.

Hook-Up
- Track getting good traction with minimum spin.

Hyfax
- A durable plastic type runner attached to suspension skid bottom.

Idler Wheels
- Mounted to skid frame rails and suspension. minimizes track slap.

Jack Shaft
- Driven clutch bolts to this.

Jet Needle
- Fuel metering component in carburetor. Used to fine-tune mid range performance.

Keel
- Molded in ski bottom for control.

Limiter Strap
- Adjusts front of skid frame height.

Liquid Cooled
- Engine cooled with antifreeze.

Long Track
- A track usually 136", 141" to 156"

Long Track Kit
- Kit used to convert short track to long track.

Main Jet
- Made of brass carb jet. Regulates fuel 3/4 to top end at max throttle.

Melt Down
- Pistons so hot the tops melt, showing a hole.

Moguls
- Large bumps and holes on a trail.

Needle Jet
- Carburetor jet in carb bore used to tune mid range.

Octane
- Saturated hydrocarbons, chemically produced to designate anti-knock.

O.E.M.
- Original Equipment Manufacturer.

Off the Pipe
- Engine falling off its power.

Over Steer
- Skis biting too much,

Pilots
- In carb, regulates starting and idle.

Pivoting
- Sled squirms in middle.

Point & Shoot
- A machine able to go anywhere in a late season because of a solid snow base.

Powder Skis
- Skis made wide for floatation, approximately 7.5". Some ski skins to 10".

Power Band
- The rpm range where the engine is making useable power, usually from engagement rpm to peak power rpm.

Pre-Load
- Spring tension before weight is applied.

Profile
- Refers to shapes of drive clutch weights.

Push
- Ski pushes snow when turning.

Radius Rods
- Connect trailing arms to bulk head.

Ratcheting
- Noise heard if track or drive chain is too loose.

Recoil
- Pulls starter rope back into housing.

Rocker Skis
- Keel of ski shaped like a rocker.

Roll On
- Power that builds consistently smooth without abrupt wack.

Roller Cam
- Replaces cam buttons on back clutch with rollers, for less friction.

Rolling Resistance
- Reduced friction throughout the sled.

Scrub
- The change in ski stance as front suspension goes through its travel.

Short Track
- Track usually 114" to 121" in length.

Side Hilling
- Riding crossways on a hill other than with angle. Riding a sled on one ski on its side on a hill.

Silencers
- Replaces stock muffler for lighter weight and louder sound.

Ski Loops
- Grab handles on ski fronts.

Ski Stance
- Ski width from centre to centre of ski spindles.

Skid Frame
- Encompasses rear suspension parts. Bolts into the tunnel. Four bolts hold the rear suspension in the tunnel in most sleds.

Skid Plate
- Rivets to belly pan and protects from damage.

Ski Skins
- Attaches to bottom of skis for floatation.

Snow Cross
- Snowmobile racing on motor cross track on snow.

Snow Blindness
- Eyes become bloodshot and hurt from snow and sun glare.

Solar Fleece - Polar Fleece
- Man-made very warm fiber.

Sound>ROO-ROO-ROO
- Out of true track drivers or bent drive axle.

Spindles
- Front suspension part connects ski to steering arm.

Studs
- Put in track for better traction.

Sway Bar
- Holds and stabilizes front end of sled (in front suspension).

Tachometer
- Shows engine RPM.

Tether Switch
- Attaches to rider and sled. If rider falls off, engine will stop.

Toe Out
- Wider at ski fronts than a the back of skis.

Torque
- Twisting force caused by rotation.

Trail Skis
- Approximately 5.5" wide with aggressive carbides.

Tread Plates
- Adds grip to running boards.

Triple
- Three Cylinders

Triple-Triple
- Three cylinders with three pipes installed.

Tripmeter
- For your mileage read on each trip.

Tuned Pipe
- Designed for more horsepower and tuned for the engine.

Tunnel
- Rear suspension and skid frame bolts in here.

Turbo
- Forced air into engine for greatly increased horsepower.

Twin
- Two cylinders.

Understeer
- Skis not turning the sled.

Up Shift
- Sled moves into a higher gear ratio.

Windage Plate
- Attaches to driven clutch to reduce air drag.

ABBREVIATIONS

A.B.
- Avalanche Beacon

A.C.M.
- Acceleration Control Modulator

A.R.C.
- Advanced Ride Control

A.W.S.
- Articulated Wishbone Suspension

C.C.S.O.
- Canadian Council of Snowmobile Organization

C.R.C.
- Controlled Roll Centre

D.A.J.
- Dial A Jet

D.P.M.
- Digital Performance Management

D.S.A.
- Direct Shock Action

E.F.I.
- Electronic Fuel Injection

E.G.T.
- Exhaust Gas Temperature

E.P.A.
- Environmental Protection Agency

E.T.T.
- Extended Travel Tunnel

G.P.S.
- Global Positioning System

H.A.C.
- High Altitude Compensator

H.P.
- Horse Power

I.F.S.
- Independent Front Suspension

M.A.C.
- Mikuni Altitude Compensator

O.E.M.
- Original Equipment Manufacturer

P.T.O.
- Power Take Off

R.A.V.E.
- Rotax Adjustable Variable Exhaust

R.P.M.
- Revolutions Per Minute

S.C.
- Smart Carb

S.C. 10
- Super Comfort 10"

T.D.C.
- Top Dead Centre

T.R.A.
- Total Range Adjustable Clutch

T.S.L.
- Torque Sensing Link

FIRST AID FOR EMERGENCIES

St. John Ambulance

The following information is presented as a public service.
Neither Fun on Snow Publications nor St. John Ambulance assume any liability for the actions recommended.
Revised in conformity with "Standards and Guidelines for C.P.R." (1994)

INTRODUCTION

"First Aid Emergencies" is a guide to the individual with little or no knowledge of First Aid. This guide provides you with step-by-step procedures on what to do in an emergency. It is not a First Aid course. The primary objectives of First Aid are: to save lives, prevent conditions from worsening and promote recovery.

Be prepared to face your next emergency:
  • take a First Aid course that includes CPR (cardiovascular resuscitation) and keep your certificate current.
  • have a well stocked First Aid Kit (including syrup of Ipecac) in the home, and know how to use it, and
  • ensure children and baby-sitter know your emergency ambulance number.

PREVENTION IS BETTER THAN CURE

CONTENTS

SNOWMOBILING

1/ Safety

Before starting any First Aid, always ensure the area is safe
A. For yourself   B. For the casualty

2/ How to call your Emergency Ambulance Number

A. Call 911

1. Keep calm
2. Speak clearly
3. Answer questions

B. State type of emergency
C. Give location of emergency
D. Confirm that the dispatcher has all necessary information before you hang up.

3/ Unconsciousness

A. **Check for unconsciousness** (fig -1)
   1. Call out to casualty.
   2. Gently tap shoulders.
B. **If no response**

Fig -1

1. **Send for an ambulance.** If alone and a phone is nearby but out of sight, place casualty in recovery position (fig 2) before leaving to call for an ambulance.

Fig -2

Recovery position

IF INJURIES ARE NOT SUSPECTED

Fig -3

2. **Position casualty face up**
3. **Open the airway** (fig -3)
(a) Use one hand to tilt the forehead
(b) Use the other hand to lift the chin

Open the Airway

Fig -4

4. **Check for breathing (fig -4)**
(a) Look for chest movement
(b) Listen for breathing
(c) Feel for breath on your cheek

Assess Breathing

IF INJURIES ARE SUSPECTED

2. Check breathing without moving the casualty
(a) Look for chest movement
(b) Listen for breathing
(c) Feel for breath on your cheek

IF NOT BREATHING

3. **Position Casualty face up** - minimize neck movement

Opening the Airway with Jaw Thrust

4. **Open the airway and check breathing**   Fig -5
(a) lift both sides of the jaw without moving neck (fig -5)
(b) **Look, listen and feel for breathing**

---

5. If casualty is not breathing, begin Artificial Respiration (Section 4)

6. Place in recovery position if... (fig -2)
   (a) Unconscious casualty is breathing and injuries **are not** suspected
   (b) Breathing is noisy (gurgling or snoring sounds)
   (c) Casualty starts to vomit
   (d) Casualty is bleeding from the mouth
   (e) You must leave the casualty unattended

4/ Artificial Respiration

ADULT CASUALTY	CHILD CASUALTY	INFANT CASUALTY
A. Give 2 breaths: 1. Open the airway. 2. Cover casualty's mouth with yours and pinch nostrils. (fig -6) 3. Give enough air to make chest rise. Fig -6 **B. If air does not go in, perform steps for choking adult.** **C. Check carotid pulse (fig -7)** for 5 - 10 seconds. - if pulse present, give 1 breath every 5 seconds Fig -7 - if pulse absent, START CPR.	**A. Give 2 breaths:** 1. Open the airway. 2. Cover child's mouth with your mouth and pinch nostrils. (fig -8) Fig -8 3. Give just enough air to make chest rise. **B. If air does not go in, perform steps for choking child .** **C. Check carotid pulse (fig -9)** for 5 - 10 seconds. • if pulse present, give 1 breath every 3 seconds. • if pulse absent, START CPR. Fig -9	**A. Give 2 breaths:** 1. Open the airway. 2. Cover infant's mouth and nose with your mouth. (fig -10) 3. Give just enough air to make chest rise. Fig -10 **B. If air does not go in, perform steps for choking infant.** **C. Check brachial pulse** for 5 - 10 seconds. (fig -11) • if pulse present, give 1 breath every 3 seconds. • if pulse absent, START CPR. Fig -11

5/ Cardiopulmonary Resuscitation (CPR)

PERFORM CPR ONLY IF THE CASUALTY IS:

A. Unconscious
B. Not breathing
C. Pulseless

ADULT CPR	CHILD CPR	INFANT CPR
A. Check the carotid pulse for 5-10 seconds. If absent: **B.** Do CPR compressions: (fig -12) 1. Place heel of one hand on lower half of breastbone in centre of chest. Fig -12 2. Place heel of other hand on top of first hand. 3. Press straight down to compress chest 1.5 - 2 inches. (3.8 to 5 cm) Rate: 15 compressions in 9 seconds. Fig -13 **C.** Give 2 breaths after every 15 compressions. **D.** Re-check pulse and breathing after 1 minute of CPR. (fig -13) **E.** If pulse is still absent, continue CPR until help arrives.	**A.** Check the carotid pulse for 5-10 seconds. If absent: **B.** Do CPR compressions (fig -14) 1. Tilt back forehead with heel of one hand. 2. Place heel of other hand on lower half of breast bone in centre of chest. Fig -14 3. Press straight down to compress chest 1 - 1.5 inches (2.8 to 3.8 cm) Rate: 5 compressions in 3 seconds. **C.** Give 1 breath after every 5 compressions. **D.** Re-check pulse and breathing after 1 minute of CPR. (fig -15) Fig -15 **E.** If pulse is still absent, continue CPR until help arrives.	**A.** Check the brachial pulse for 5-10 seconds. If absent: **B.** Do CPR compressions: (fig -16) 1. Tilt back forehead with heel of one hand. 2. Place 2 fingers of other hand in centre of chest, one finger width below nipple line. Fig -16 3. Press straight down to compress chest 1/2 - 1 inch Rate: 5 compressions in 3 seconds or less. **C.** Give 1 breath after every 5 compressions. **D.** Re-check pulse Fig -17 and breathing after 1 minute of CPR. (fig -17) **E.** If pulse is still absent, continue CPR until help arrives.

6/ CHOKING

CONSCIOUS ADULT OR CHILD

A. Ask: "Are you choking?" (fig -18)
If casualty can speak or cough, airway is open enough to force out obstructing object. Fig -18

B. If casualty <u>CAN</u> speak or cough
1. Reassure and encourage coughing
2. Do not hit on back.

C. If casualty <u>CANNOT</u> speak or cough
1. Stand behind casualty, locate hip bones and wrap your arms around waist.
2. Make a fist with one hand and place above navel, at hip level. Grasp fist with other hand. (fig -19)
3. Thrust inward and upward into abdomen.
4. Repeat abdominal thrusts until airway is clear or casualty becomes unconscious.
5. If casualty becomes unconscious, follow steps in UNCONSCIOUS ADULT OR CHILD. Fig -19

CONSCIOUS INFANT

If obstruction is due to upper respiratory tract infection (cough, cold, etc.), do not give First Aid for choking. Get immediate medical attention.

A. Determine if infant is choking on foreign substance. Fig -21

B. Give 5 back blows: (fig -21)
1. Place infant's head <u>lower</u> than trunk.
2. Support head.
3. Give 5 back blows between shoulder blades using heel of one hand.

C. Give 5 chest thrusts: (fig -22)
1. Turn infant face up, keeping head lower than trunk.
2. Support head.
3. Place 2 fingers on breastbone, 1 finger width below nippleline, and give 5 chest thrusts. Fig -22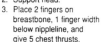

D. Continue back blows and chest thrusts until object is removed or infant becomes unconscious.

E. If infant becomes unconscious, follow steps in UNCONSCIOUS INFANT.

UNCONSCIOUS ADULT OR CHILD

A. Attempt Artificial Respiration. If air does not go in...

B. Reposition head, ensure good seal and try again. If air still does not go in...

C. Give 5 abdominal thrusts: (fig -20)
1. Straddle casualty's legs.
2. Locate waist. Place heel of one hand in centre of abdomen just above belly button. Place heel of other hand on top.
3. Give 5 quick inward and upward thrusts.

D. Inspect the mouth for foreign material.
1. Grasp lower jaw. Lift jaw forward and inspect mouth.
Adult only: insert finger of other hand deep into mouth and sweep to remove foreign material.

E. Open airway and attempt to give 2 full breaths. Repeat steps C-E until successful. Fig -20

F. When obstruction clears, follow steps in Section 4: ARTIFICIAL RESPIRATION.

UNCONSCIOUS INFANT

A. Attempt Artificial Respiration. If air does not go in...

B. Reposition head, ensure good seal and try again. If air still does not go in... Fig -23

C. Give 5 back blows: (fig -23)
1. Place infants head <u>lower</u> than trunk.
2. Support head.
3. Give 5 back blows between shoulder blades using heel of one hand.

D. Give 5 chest thrusts: (fig -24)
1. Turn infant face up, keeping head lower than trunk and support head.
2. Place 2 fingers on the breastbone just below nippleline.
3. Give 5 sharp thrusts.

E. Inspect the mouth.
1. Grasp the lower jaw. Lift jaw forward and inspect mouth. Fig -24
2. Only if foreign material is seen, sweep the mouth with little finger of other hand.

F. Open airway and attempt to give 2 breaths. Repeat steps C-F until successful.

G. When obstruction clears, follow steps in Section 4: ARTIFICIAL RESPIRATION.

7/ Heart Attack

A. Warning signals of heart attack may include:

1. Feeling of heavy pressure or squeezing pain in chest, arms or jaw.
2. Shortness of breath, pale skin, sweating and weakness.
3. Nausea and vomiting.
4. Abdominal discomfort with indigestion and belching.
5. Apprehension or fright.
6. Denial of impending heart attack.

B. Action When you suspect a heart attack:

1. Help casualty to rest, sitting or lying in most comfortable position.
2. Assist casualty to take the correct dose of medication if prescribed for his condition.
3. Ensure prompt medical attention by calling your emergency ambulance number.
4. Reassure casualty "Help is on the way."
5. Loosen collar, belt and other tight clothing.
6. Keep casualty quiet but avoid physical restraint.

8/ Bleeding

Serious bleeding may occur with deep cuts and severed blood vessels.

A. Ensure safety.
B. Send for an ambulance when bleeding is severe.
C. Control bleeding. (fig -25)
1. Assist casualty to sit or lie down.
2. Remove clothing to expose extent of wound.
3. Cover with sterile dressing or clean cloth.
4. Apply firm pressure directly over the dressings. If dressings are not available, have casualty use own hand to apply pressure.
5. Elevate limb if a fracture is not suspected.

Fig -25

Direct pressure
Elevation
Rest

6. Apply a firm bandage.
7. If blood soaks through, apply additional dressings and bandage more firmly.

D. Broken bone, glass or objects protruding through skin (fig -26).

1. Do not remove embedded objects.
2. Cover wound with clean dressings.
3. Apply pressure close to wound but not pressing on broken bone or object.
4. Maintain pressure and prevent movement of

Fig -26

object by applying bulky pads around the object. Bandage pads in place.

E. Nosebleeds
1. Seat casualty with head tilted forward.
2. Pinch nostrils firmly for 10 minutes.
3. Avoid nose blowing for several hours.
4. If bleeding persists, call an ambulance.

9/ Bone and Joint Injuries

Suspect a broken bone if injured limb is painful or swollen or shows deformity.

A. Ensure safety.
1. Do not move casualty except for reasons of safety.
B. Call an ambulance.
C. Check breathing.
D. Control severe bleeding.

E. When in doubt, treat all bone and joint injuries as broken bones.
1. To relieve pain, apply cold (not heat) to injuries of bones and joints.
2. Support limb with your hands to prevent movement.
F. For neck and back injuries
1. Warn casualty not to move.
2. Support head and neck by hand in position found to prevent movement.
3. Keep body still until help arrives.

10/ Eye Injuries

A. Call an ambulance for all serious eye injuries.
B. Chemicals in eye.
1. Wash eye immediately with large amounts of cool, running water for at least 15 minutes.
C. Foreign object in eye.
1. Never rub eye and do not try to remove embedded foreign objects.
2. Cover eye lightly with bandage.

D. Puncture wounds.
1. Help casualty to lie down in face up position. Caution not to move.
2. Cover injured eye with clean dressing and secure lightly with bandage.

11/ Severe Burns and Scalds

A. Ensure safety.
B. Call ambulance for severe burns or scalds.
C. For burns or scalds caused by fire, hot solids, hot liquids or sun:
1. Cool affected part with cool water.
2. Remove rings and bracelets before part starts to swell.
3. Cover burn with clean cloth and secure lightly with bandage.
4. Ensure hospital treatment for deep burns and scalds of areas larger than a quarter.
5. DO NOT breathe on, cough on, or touch burns.
6. DO NOT break blisters.

7. DO NOT remove clothing stuck to burn.
8. DO NOT apply medications, ointments, or greasy substances to burn.
D. For burns caused by dry chemicals:
1. Brush off dry chemicals.
2. Flood with running water for 15 to 20 minutes.
3. Cover burn with clean cloth and secure lightly with bandage.
E. For electrical burns:
1. Turn off electricity before touching casualty.
2. Check for breathing and pulse.
3. Cover burn with clean cloth and secure lightly with bandage.

12/ Heat Exposure (Hyperthermia)

A. Definition: High body temperature due to overexertion or high temperature.
B. Treatment:
1. Remove casualty to a cool area.
2. If unconscious:

(a) Call an ambulance.
(b) Ensure breathing and pulse.
(c) Place in recovery position.

3. If conscious, give fluids to drink.
4. If hot, sponge with cool water.

13/ Cold Exposure (Hypothermia)

A. Definition: Loss of body heat.
B. Treatment:
1. If unconscious:

(a) Call an ambulance.
(b) Ensure breathing and pulse.
(c) Remove from cold environment; protect from further cooling.
(d) Do not attempt to rewarm casualty.

2. If conscious:

(a) Remove from cold environment.
(b) Remove wet clothing.
(c) Give warm, sweet drinks (no alcohol)
(d) Warm slowly by wrapping in prewarmed sleeping bag, blankets or warm clothing.

14/ Poisoning

A. In all cases:
1. Ensure safety.
2. Identify poison and container, if possible.
3. Phone **Poison Control Centre** **682-5050** Outside GVRD 1+800+567-8911.
4. Call an ambulance. Send container and contents with casualty to hospital.

B. Inhaled poisons such as exhaust fumes.
1. Remove source of fumes.
2. Move casualty to fresh air.
3. Check breathing and pulse.
4. Give artificial respiration or CPR as required.

C. Poisons in contact with skin or eyes.
1. Flood area with a gentle stream of cool running water for at least 15 minutes.
2. Continue flooding area until ambulance takes over.
3. Remove contaminated clothing.
4. Do not use chemical antidotes.

D. For swallowed household chemical poisons:

1. Conscious casualty

(a) Phone your Poison Control Centre or (604) 682-5050 in Vancouver, BC. Follow their advice on first aid.
(b) Only induce vomiting on advice of **Poison Control Centre or Physician**. If advised, use Syrup of Ipecac (available without prescription at pharmacies). If poison is hydrocarbon or corrosive, do **NOT** induce vomiting.
(c) To avoid inhalation of vomit, place casualty's head lower than body in recovery position.

2. If Unconscious

(a) Call an ambulance.
(b) Ensure breathing and pulse.
(c) Place casualty in recovery position.
(d) Do **NOT** induce vomiting.

INDEX